David Kline

Great Possessions

An Amish Farmer's Journal

Foreword by Wendell Berry

The Wooster Book Company

Wooster ❦ Ohio

2001

Library of Congress Cataloging-in-Publication Data
Kline, David.
Great possessions : an Amish farmer's journal / by David Kline.
p.   cm.
1. Nature.   2. Seasons.   I. Title.
QH81.K66   1989
508—dc20   89-16018

ISBN 1-888683-22-8

The Wooster Book Company
205 West Liberty Street
Wooster, Ohio 44691
www.woosterbook.com

For my family

Contents

Acknowledgments

I am deeply grateful to my entire family for their understanding, encouragement, and generous offers to do the evening milking without my help so that I would have an hour of uninterrupted time to meet an editor's deadline. I am especially grateful to Elsie, whose unflagging support and counsel more than once restored my confidence; to Dominique Gioia for her skilled editing, sound judgment, and the enthusiasm that made this book possible; to Elmo Stoll for his encouragement, advice, and almost limitless patience; and to my parents and the late C. F. Zuercher for opening the door to the natural world for me.

These essays first appeared in *Family Life* magazine. The introduction was presented, in somewhat different form, in a talk at the North American Conference on Christianity and Ecology, North Webster, Indiana.

Foreword

The essays collected in this book were written over several years as articles for the Amish magazine, *Family Life*. They belong to the tradition of "the natural history essay," a kind of writing that comes of the delight that humans take in knowing about the creatures of nature. David Kline knows this tradition, and he is comfortable in it, for he has experienced fully the delight that it springs from. He has lived and written under the influence of the charming knowledge that his small farm is the home of many fascinating creatures that he did not put there, but that he may choose, as he does, to make welcome. When he tells us about these creatures, he is speaking both as an alert and perceptive observer and as a careful reader. His experience is supported by his reading, his reading by his experience.

But these essays go beyond their genre, and thus greatly increase their value, by showing us also a kind of life in which delight in the wild creatures is ordinary. They are written, not just from knowledge, but from familiarity. And that distinction is vital, for David's acquaintance with the animals, birds, plants, and insects that he writes about is literally familiar: they are part of his family life. Knowing these creatures is one of his family's entertainments, and one of its bonds.

The Old Order Amish communities, of one of which David is a member, have preserved profound connections between things that conventional American society has normally separated. David's way of life, for example, does not divide the life of the mind from the life of the body. That he lives by physical work has not denied him an active mental life, nor has it denied him both physical and mental delight. In the same way, his work does not involve or imply the rigid division of human domestic life from the life of nature that is now normal in the industrial economy.

David's life—informed as it is by the Amish reverence for the natural world and the stewardship everywhere implicit in Amish farming—makes a union of economy and ecology. It does this by a complex pattern of small attentions and small courtesies, such as timing a hay cutting to permit bobolink fledglings to leave the nest.

This sort of consideration is made possible by the diversity and the propriety of scale that belong to traditional small-farm agriculture, and by a margin of spare time or of leisure that surrounds such agriculture. This is the leisure of the ungreedy self-employed. How many factory or office employees are ever caught up with their work and able on their own initiative to take a few days off? And yet David writes of such a liberty as a matter of course: "With the hectic pace of spring plowing and planting behind us, we now have a week or more to pursue other spring pleasures." The pleasures he is talking about are the pleasures of natural history. And he is most likely to pursue these pleasures of his leisure, not in some "getaway" or vacation place, but on his farm and in his neighborhood, the places of his work. It is equally important to notice that these pleasures are pursued also in the midst of work. Time and again, David tells us of something he observed while he was plowing or mowing.

And so we see that another unity that the Amish have preserved is that of work and pleasure. The lives of fellow creatures and our delight in those lives are great possessions. And these are secured and made available by great possessions that are cultural.

This book announces on every page that the world is good, an article of faith that is here brought to rest upon experience. That David Kline and his neighbors look at the world and find it good, and that they honor its goodness in their daily work, permits them to say something that, after a decade of severe agricultural depression, is at once astonishing and profoundly reassuring: "Farming is good."

Wendell Berry

Introduction

Not too long ago, the editor of a back-to-the-land magazine asked me to write something on small-scale diversified traditional farming—on the advantages of such a way of life, he suggested, and also the disadvantages. This bothered me all summer. Quite honestly, I couldn't think of any disadvantages.

What are the lessons, if any, I wondered, to be learned from our way of farming? Is it a way of farming that preserves the soil, the water, the air, the wildlife, the families that work the land, and the surrounding communities? In other words, are we proper caretakers or stewards of God's Creation? Are we in harmony with God and nature?

To write about Amish agriculture is to write about traditional agriculture, an agriculture dating back to eighteenth-century Europe, handed down from generation to generation and yet with innovations and improvements constantly added along the way. The Amish are not necessarily against modern technology. We have simply chosen not to be controlled by it.

Amish farming is sometimes best looked at by someone outside the community, for many of our practices are so traditional, having been handed down from parents to children for so many generations, that the reasons are almost forgotten. For example, the rotation of our field crops here in eastern Ohio works so well it's seldom questioned. This is a four- or five-year rotation, which means a given field will be in corn every fourth or fifth year. (I should mention that the type of

Amish farming I'm talking about is practiced by our people in Ohio, northern Indiana, southern Michigan, and possibly southern Ontario. Amish communities in other states may differ somewhat in their ways of farming. Yet there are many similarities, I'm sure.)

In our rotation, corn is followed by oats. In the fall after the oats are harvested, the stubble is plowed, and wheat is sowed; the wheat is then top-seeded the following March or April with legume seeds. Seeding is done with a hand-cranked or horn-type seeder and usually on frozen ground, where the early-nesting horned larks nest. The dropping seeds cause enough disturbance to flush the incubating bird. The nest is then easily found.

After the wheat is cut and threshed in July the stubble is mowed and, almost miraculously, the wheatfield converts to a hayfield. The next spring and summer several cuttings of hay are made and then the hayfield is pastured in the fall. (In a five-year rotation the field remains in hay for two years.) During the winter the old sod is liberally covered with strawy manure. In late winter or early spring the sod is plowed and in May planted again to corn and the rotation or cycle begins again.

What chemicals must be bought and added to raise a decent crop of corn in a field like this? None, except for the fungicide with which the seed corn is usually treated before we buy it. With the legumes converting free nitrogen to the soil from the air plus ten to fifteen tons of manure per acre supplying thirty pounds of nitrogen per ton in addition to other plant foods, no extra fertilizer is needed. (I should add that the majority of Amish farmers apply one hundred to one hundred and fifty pounds of a low-analysis fertilizer—such as 5-20-20—per acre as a starter plant food. I know quite a few farmers, though, who don't use any purchased fertilizer for corn and raise an excellent crop.)

Likewise, no insecticides are needed in this field because

with corn following hay there are no crop-damaging insects. We have never used a soil insecticide. Rarely, in wet weather, slugs will cause some problems in corn planted in plowed sod. But the first cultivation destroys their burrows, and by the time the slow creatures get geared up for their next attack, the corn has outgrown the stage where it can be damaged.

The cultivating, besides taking care of the slugs, also takes care of the weeds. Most Amish farmers are not what you would consider pure organic farmers. Many will use some herbicides in corn to help control problem weeds and grasses. But the Amish usage of herbicides is small in comparison to that in conventional continuous corn farming because the need is small. One year my neighbor's total herbicide cost was $11— not per acre, but for *all* his corn. He band-sprays a small amount on the row. Between the rows he gets the weeds with his cultivator.

Most of us aren't too concerned if there are some weeds and grasses in our corn. In fact, I want some there. Occasionally we get summer thundershowers that dump several inches of rain in half an hour or less, which is more than even the most absorbent soil can take. During storms like this we depend on a smattering of quack grass and on sod waterways to hold the topsoil.

According to researchers at Oberlin College, the strength of our topsoil can be attributed to the tilth of our soils. Their study shows that our traditionally horse-worked farms absorb almost seven times more water before becoming saturated than the conventional no-tilled farms.

Presently no-till farming with its dependence on vast amounts of chemicals is being touted by the experts as the way to guarantee green fields forever. What they fail to say is that these green fields will be strangely silent—gone will be the bobolink, the meadowlark, and the sweet song of the vesper sparrow in the twilight.

A young farmer friend related to me how thrilled he was last spring when two pairs of bobolinks took up residence in one of his sod fields, a field that was to be planted to corn using the no-till method. He hesitated somewhat to spray the field, but then he remembered the film the Chevron salesman had shown the previous winter indicating that no-till improves the habitat for wildlife. He sprayed the paraquat and soon after, the bobolinks disappeared. Since he didn't hear their cheerful flight songs from nearby fields he's quite positive the birds perished.

Another disadvantage with no-till is that the farmers' options are severely limited. Should there be too much or too little rain—conditions which often reduce the effectiveness of many herbicides—or an invasion of army worms or slugs, the farmer can't cultivate and must instead come back with more pesticides. I was recently told that during late spring and early summer every raindrop in the eastern corn belt contains minute parts of *Lasso*, a popular corn herbicide and suspected carcinogen. Can you love your neighbor and do this?

But, to champions of agribusiness, that is progress. And profits . . . for them. One Soil Conservation Service (SCS) board member made the comment, "The Amish minds are too 'unscientific' to understand the intricacies of proper soil management, so they should learn to rely on outside experts for advice." At another farmer-advisor meeting when the discussion drifted around to no-till, the expert, educated in the atmosphere of a land-grant college where the jargon revolves around "input," "output," "acre-eaters," "work-is-drudgery," "cash flow," and "bottom line," made the remark, "No-till sure beats plowing."

Here it is then, the thorn in my side—I never did care for Faulkner's *Plowman's Folly*—I enjoy plowing. Just this past year the SCS technician told me, in all seriousness, that if I'd join the no-till crowd I'd be freed from plowing, and then my son or I could work in a factory. He insinuated that the extra income (increased cash flow) would in some way improve the quality of our lives.

I failed to get his point. Should we, instead of working the land traditionally, which requires the help of most family members, send our sons to work in factories to support Dad's farming habit? Should we be willing to relinquish a nonviolent way of farming that was developed in Europe and fine-tuned in America (by what Wendell Berry calls "generations of experience")? Should we give up the kind of farming that has been proven to preserve communities and land and is ecologically and spiritually sound for a way that is culturally and environmentally harmful?

And there are the pleasures of plowing—plowing encompasses more than just turning the soil. Although I can't fully describe the experience, it is like being a part of a whole. In early spring, my son and I, each with a team as eager to be out as we are, turn the mellow soil, feeling its coolness and tilth. We take pleasure in the transient water pipits and pectoral sandpipers feeding on the freshly turned earth abounding with life. As we rest the teams, I listen to the joys and uncertainties of teenage years.

Maybe I'm blind, but no matter which angle I look from, I fail to see any drudgery in this work. And I am convinced that if one farms carefully, soil erosion need not be a problem.

Several springs ago—actually it was in late winter—following a week of unseasonably warm weather, Dennis Weaver, our neighbor to the south, couldn't resist the urge any longer and started plowing. I wasn't aware of it until, while walking to the barn, I suddenly caught the aroma of newly turned earth. I stood there, closed my eyes, and reveled in it: the promise of spring.

With no-till I would have the means to farm his fifty tillable acres, in addition to my own, and he could be "free" to work off the farm. I know I wouldn't be able to do the excellent farming he is doing now, and I would miss the rich fragrance of his fertile soil. But more than that, I would miss my neighbor.

There are lessons to be learned from small-scale diversified farming. By working and farming the way the Amish traditionally have done, we make our place more attractive to wildlife. Should we be removed from the land and our farm turned into a "wildlife area," I'm almost positive that the numbers and species of wildlife would dwindle.

Naturally, this doesn't mean that farming to the roadsides and cleaning and spraying fencerows, as even some Amish do, particularly in communities of high land prices, can be done without ill effect to wild things. Along with a diversity of crops and livestock and minimal use of pesticides, there should be some overgrown fencerows—which harbor a host of wild creatures from catbirds to cottontails—brushy woods' edges, sod waterways, trees around the farm buildings, an orchard, lots of flowers (both garden and wild), maybe a patch of prairie.

Gary Nabhan wrote in *The Desert Smells Like Rain* about two Sonora Desert oases, the first of which, in Arizona, began to die when the Park Service turned it into a bird sanctuary and, in an effort to preserve it for wildlife, removed the Indians who farmed and lived there. The other oasis, across the Mexican border, has long been tended by a village of Papago Indians and is thriving. An ornithologist found twice as many species of birds there as he found at the bird sanctuary in Arizona.

Last week our family made a survey of nesting birds around our farm buildings. This doesn't include the bobolinks, redwings, meadowlarks, and sparrows in the fields, nor does it include the vireos, tanagers, warblers, and thrushes in the woods or the rough-winged swallows and kingfishers along the creek. We came up with over eighteen hundred young of thirteen species fledged within two hundred feet of our house. This included a colony of 250 pairs of cliff swallows along the barn eaves. As Mr. Nabhan's Indian friend said, "That's because those birds, they come where the people are. When the people live and work in a place, and plant their seeds, and water their trees, the birds go live with them. They like those places, there's plenty to eat, and that's when we are friends to them."

But we farm the way we do because we believe in nurturing and supporting all our community—that includes people as well as land and wildlife. By farming and living independently of electricity the Amish are not contributing, at least not directly, I hope, to the destruction of hundreds of farms and communities in southeastern Ohio where the Ohio Power Company is strip-mining coal to supply its power plants on the Ohio River. Along with the destroyed farms, the mammoth power plants spew out sulfur dioxides that contribute to the acid rain killing forests in the Northeast and lakes in the Adirondacks.

The Amish have traditionally maintained a scale of farming that enabled each farm to be worked by a family. Few farms have more than eighty tillable acres, which is about the maximum a father and son can easily work. If more help becomes available the operation may be expanded to include more livestock or possibly specialty crops such as vegetables. Rarely are more acres added.

Wes Jackson has said, "The pleasantness or unpleasantness of farm work depends upon scale—upon the size of the field and the size of the crop." The Amish have maintained what I like to think is a proper scale, largely by staying with the horse. The horse has restricted unlimited expansion. Not only does working with horses limit farm size, but horses are ideally suited to family life. With horses you unhitch at noon to water and feed the teams and then the family eats what we still call dinner. While the teams rest there is usually time for a short nap. And because God didn't create the horse with headlights, we don't work nights.

We have seventy tillable acres, which is maybe ten acres

more than the average farm in our community. We couldn't take care of more. With this size farm there is usually something to do, yet we're never overwhelmed by work. I confess, though, that this past July we came close to being overwhelmed. Rain delayed the second cutting of hay and then when the rains quit we had hay to harvest, wheat to thresh, and oats to cut, all at once. Under normal conditions, though, the work is spread out from spring to fall.

The field work begins in March with the plowing of sod. This is leisurely work, giving the horses plenty of time to become conditioned, and giving us my version of what the Quakers call quiet time: a time to listen to God and His Creation as we participate in the unfolding of spring. Wendell Berry writes in *Getting Along with Nature*: "A proper human sound . . . is one that allows other sounds to be heard"—and plowing sod is such a human sound. We hear the creaking of the harness and the popping of alfalfa roots, as well as the tinkling song of the horned lark and the lisping of the migrating water pipits. A wonderful time.

April is for plowing cornstalks and sowing oats, for spring beauties and lovely hepatica.

In May, we plant the corn, turn the cows and horses out to pasture, and revel in warblers and morel mushrooms.

With hay making in June come the strawberries, shortcakes, pies, and jams. The bird migration is over and summer settles in.

Life and work on the farm peaks in July with threshing, second-cutting hay, transparent apples, new honey, blackberries, and the first katydid.

August already hints of autumn. The whine of the silo fillers is heard throughout the land. We fill our ten-by-forty-foot silo with the help of four neighbors.

McIntosh apples and sowing wheat mean September.

October is corn harvest and cider-making and loving the

colors and serenity only October can offer. As the month draws to a close so does the field work.

The year is a never-ending adventure. What many consider recreation we enjoy on our own farm. This year we saw four firsts on the farm: our first Kentucky warbler; our first luna and imperial moths; and after waiting for over thirty years, I saw my first giant swallowtail butterfly.

The aesthetic pleasures of diversified farming are obvious. From spring through fall the colors of the fields are constantly changing. I like to look at our farm as an artist would behold his or her painting—a variation of colors and designs, never a bare spot of canvas left exposed. The bare spots on our farm, such as cow paths, are covered in November with strawy horse manure to prevent erosion. I use the manure spreader, which works fine as a mulcher. The land is now ready for the rains and storms of winter.

Probably the greatest difference between Amish farming and agribusiness is the supportive community life we have. Let me give an example. When we cut our wheat in early summer (we cut about half of a thirteen-acre field in one day), the whole family, after the evening milking, went shocking. It was one of those clear, cool June evenings. Simply perfect. Tim, our eighteen-year-old son, and I each took a row while my wife, Elsie, and ten-year-old son, Michael, took another one. Two of our daughters, Kristine, sixteen, and Ann, twelve, took the fourth row. Eight-year-old Emily carried the water jug. Row by row we worked our way across the field, the girls talking and giggling while they worked and Michael explaining in excited detail some project he had under way in the shop. When we reached the top of the hill we stood together and watched the sun slip behind a brilliant magenta-colored cloud and then sink beneath the horizon. From far to the south came the mellow whistle of an upland sandpiper. Tim said, to no one in particular, "Shocking together with the family is fun." He spoke for all of us. Then we heard voices from the next hill and saw three neighbors shocking toward us from the far end of the field. One of the girls excitedly remarked, "Seven rows at a time. That is speed." Soon all the bundles were set up in shocks and everyone came along to the house for ice cream and visiting.

The assurance and comfort of having caring neighbors is one of the reasons we enjoy our way of farming so much. Eight years ago I had an accident that required surgery and a week in the hospital. My wife tells me the first words I said to her in the recovery room were, "Get me out of here; the wheat has to be cut." Of course, she couldn't, and I need not have worried because we had neighbors.

While Dad cut the wheat with the binder, the neighbors shocked it. When our team tired my brother brought his four-horse team, and by suppertime the twelve-acre field was cut and shocked.

This year the neighbor who had been in first to help us needed help himself. Since a bout of pneumonia in July he hadn't been able to do much. So last Thursday six teams and mowers cut his eleven acres of alfalfa hay. Then on Saturday afternoon, with four teams and wagons and two hay loaders and fifteen men and about as many boys, we put the hay in his barn in less than two hours. We spent almost as much time afterward, sitting in a circle beneath the maple tree with cool drinks and fresh cookies, listening as one of the neighbors told of his recent trip west. He and a friend visited draft-horse breeders in Illinois, Iowa, and eastern Nebraska, and what a story he had to tell: of nice horses and nice people, of the worst erosion he had ever seen from the Iowa hills following eight inches of rain, and how the Iowa farmers rained invective down on our president. "Ach," he said. "All they want is more government handouts."

I couldn't help thinking of my young friend who got married last September and then bought his dad's machinery and livestock and rented the farm. He and his wife really worked on that debt. Milking by hand, selling Grade B milk, tending a good group of sows, cultivating corn twice, some three times, using no herbicides, they are nearing the end of their first year of farming on their own, and most of their debts are paid off. He didn't tell me this, he's much too humble, but he did say to me while threshing, "You know, farming is good."

Great
Possessions

Winter

Winter Visitors

After several "finger-cold" days, those of us who farm at last
accept the fact that winter is here. Throughout November we
tried to pasture the livestock every decent day we could to save
on winter feed. But now it's time to keep the animals in the barn
away from the rain and cold. In the morning when I open the
barn doors I'm enveloped by the warmth and aroma of animals
and silage—not an unpleasant sensation at all. The horses demand first attention. They stomp and carry on until given their
portion of oats and hay. By then the smaller calves begin their
clamor for breakfast. The cows, the gentle creatures, patiently
wait until last, uttering hardly a sound.

December isn't just the end of the calendar year; it's also the
end of the growing season. The green and the abundance of
summer and early autumn are gone now and are replaced by
rain and overcast skies, reminding me of a poem I learned in
school. I can't remember the author, but the first verse has
stayed with me:

> The melancholy days are come
> > The saddest of the year
> Of wailing winds and naked woods,
> > And meadows brown and sear.

December is, in a way, also the end of nature's year. The
woodchuck that has its home in the fencerow along the alfalfa
field hasn't been seen for some time now. The grizzled rodent
gorged himself on the succulent legumes, putting on layers of

fat, and disappeared down his burrow to curl up in his leaf- and grass-lined nest and sleep away the winter. To preserve energy, his body temperature drops to as low as 37 degrees, and his heart may beat only two or three times per minute.

Most of our familiar summer birds have departed for climates more to their liking. Sometime during the month, however, we can expect visitors from the north. Some have already arrived. The northern (slate-colored) juncos and tree sparrows are busy feeding on weed seeds along fencerows. As soon as the first snow covers their natural food, they'll visit the feeders and will likely stay for the duration of the winter. I have often wondered why these two species flock together in the wintertime, since they occupy completely different habitats in the summer. Whereas the juncos nest in the northern coniferous forests, the tree sparrows raise their young on the treeless tundra.

Two other sparrows that are regular winter visitors are the white-throated and the white-crowned. On their northward flight in the spring, the white-throated sings its beautiful song, which to us sounds like "pure sweet Canada, Canada, Canada." New Englanders interpret it as "old Sam Peabody, Peabody, Peabody."

Another fairly common diner at our feeder is the black-capped chickadee. The chickadee that nests in this part of Ohio is the Carolina, even though we're close to the area where both species overlap. The two are difficult to tell apart. The Carolina is noticeably smaller and has less white on the wings than the black-capped. There may be many more chickadees visiting a feeder than one might think. One feeder-watcher thought he never saw more than twenty of the small acrobats around his feeder; yet when he trapped and banded them, there were over a hundred.

Others appearing irregularly are the common redpolls, red-

and white-winged crossbills, evening grosbeaks, and pine siskins.

Around ten years ago we had a near invasion of redpolls. Not too far from our farm was a vacant pig pasture that was overgrown with lamb's-quarters gone to seed. A flock of over two hundred redpolls stayed for two weeks feeding on the abundant seeds. Since these small finches nest in stunted trees along the edge of the Canadian tundra, they seldom, if ever, see people; therefore, they didn't associate me with danger. Their fearlessness enabled me to approach within three feet of the constantly twittering birds before they would burst into flight, only to circle the field, return, and alight almost at my feet. We have never since seen redpolls. Apparently they're wintering farther north.

The red- and white-winged crossbills likewise rarely venture this far south, but when they do, these tame birds can also be closely approached as they hang upside down cracking open evergreen cones with their curved bills and feeding on the seeds. Usually the only chance we have at seeing these colorful birds is when there is a poor cone crop in the boreal forests, forcing the crossbills to travel south in search of food.

The evening grosbeaks and pine siskins also invade the United States in large numbers when the northern seed crops fail. The grosbeaks are extremely fond of sunflower seeds. The increasing popularity of bird feeding has given these gregarious birds an abundant winter food supply, and they take advantage of people's generosity. While the grosbeaks devour sunflower seeds, the siskins, like our goldfinches, feed at the thistle feeders.

A little gem of the north that visits with us fairly frequently, though not annually, is the red-breasted nuthatch. Considerably smaller than our resident white-breasted nuthatch, it has rusty red underparts and a black eye-stripe. Its call, as it clings head-down to the feeder, is higher pitched and more nasal than the white-breasted's "yank, yank."

If the winter winds bring snow and an extended period of cold, we can depend on the snow buntings to pay us a visit, looking for handouts. Individuals will come to the feeder, but the main flock prefers to feed in the fields on freshly spread manure or on cracked grains we put out for them. Along with the flashy buntings are numerous horned larks and always a few Lapland longspurs. One winter we had a small pile of moldy silage outside a barn window. Each day we spread grain for the buntings closer to the barn, until finally we had them feeding on top of the silage pile. It was quite a thrill to scratch the frost off the windowpanes and see snow buntings and Lapland longspurs only two feet away.

Last March while we were plowing sod we spotted some sparrow-sized birds unlike any we had ever seen, or so we thought. After a hurried sprint to the house for a pair of binoculars, we found, to our surprise and delight, a flock of thirty or so Lapland longspurs. Instead of their drab winter coats, the males were now displaying their dashing breeding plumage. Their black heads and breasts, white stripes from their eyes down to the sides of their breasts, and reddish brown napes made them handsome birds indeed.

Though most northern visitors are in the finch family and quite small in size, some larger birds from arctic regions also move south, notably the snowy owl and rough-legged hawk. Once in a while we have snowy owls around here, but they are much more common in the flatlands along Lake Erie and in western Ohio. The big white owls find these areas more like their arctic tundra or barren ground homes. The rough-legged hawks are more common than snowy owls in this region. Almost every year, one or two of these birds include our farm in their winter hunting range. These hawks of the open country have the habit of hovering like sparrow hawks when hunting for mice. Compared to our common redtails, the roughlegs are tame. Sometimes when feeding on a road-killed rabbit, they will not take flight when passed by a buggy.

With the passing of the winter solstice on the twenty-first, the days slowly begin to lengthen and, as the saying goes, "the cold begins to strengthen." We settle in for winter. With the front porch stacked high with seasoned wood, now is the time for visits with friends, stories and games for the children, and popcorn, cider, and good books beside warm fires. Really, December is not a bad month at all. Though there are now more barn chores to do, work has slowed down, giving us more time to enjoy sharing our place on earth with visitors from the tundra and boreal forests of Canada.

A Winter Walk

It snowed the night before last and ended yesterday around noon. Now a pure white blanket four inches deep covers the countryside. After breakfast I set out to see what my wild neighbors have been up to.

Few things are so exhilarating as a winter walk when the temperature is in the teens or low twenties. There's enough bite in the air to keep you wanting to move and yet not enough cold to cause discomfort, and many creatures will have written a tale in the snow with their tracks. Ernest Thompson Seton called animal tracks "the oldest known writing on earth."

The first sign I saw as I crossed the cornfield on my way to the woods was field mouse tracks. The trails of the tiny voles would disappear near a cornstalk only to reappear several feet away to continue their journey. I have often wondered if the mice are searching for food or only frolicking in the newness of the snow. Whatever the reason, their adventuresome spirit is often their downfall. The rough-legged hawk perched on a nearby locust tree frequently dines on the little rodents. And at night the owls are watching the fields.

Leaving the cornfield, I was crossing the pasture when I came upon the doglike track of a red fox. I followed the track, which traveled in a straight, purposeful way, and as it neared a fencerow it was joined by a similar spoor, probably that of its mate. I left the tracks when they turned to the north, because I wanted to set my footprints to the west. Walking along the fencerow, I surprised a mixed flock of juncos, tree and song sparrows feeding in the safety of the brambles. Though the flock stayed ahead of me I noticed one larger bird that turned out to be a white-crowned sparrow.

For the beginning bird-watcher winter is a good time to be out. Practically all of the thirty-some species that can be seen around here on an average winter day are easy to identify. The most difficult to distinguish would be the Carolina and black-capped chickadees. These two almost identical species are tough for even experienced birders to tell apart. But many of the other wintertime birds such as the cardinals, bluejays, tufted titmice, and mourning doves would be difficult to confuse with anything else. At least when compared to a woods full of warblers on a May morning.

Continuing through the woods with its patchwork of squirrel tracks, I came to another pair of footprints much like the red fox's yet noticeably different. The prints were more cat-like, and instead of running straight meandered across logs, over stumps, and through briar patches. Gray fox. What seemed to be the tracks of a half dozen of the sly animals had actually been made by only one pair. They had covered every part of the woods on their nighttime jaunt. Cottontail tracks were scarce.

I cut across a wheatfield and here, too, I found the tracks of a gray fox, likely in pursuit of mice, whose footmarks were everywhere. I saw where one wheatfield mouse met his waterloo—not a fox but a winged enemy. According to the signs in the snow, the owl had lunged for the mouse and missed, because for four or five feet the tiny creature's tracks weren't hops but mighty leaps, obviously made by a very frightened mouse. Then there was another plowed-up mark in the snow where it all ended. What was surprising to me were the impressions of the predator's wingtips in the snow. They looked too small for a screech owl, so maybe there is a saw-whet owl in the neighborhood.

At last I reached my destination, a field of around six acres that is reverting to woodland. At its edge I was startled as a covey of bobwhites burst from the snow-covered weeds to disappear into the cover of the field. This field is now growing up with ash, tulip poplar, maple, and oak trees, in addition to a fair number of wild apples and hawthorns. The latter two along with the numerous blackberries will eventually die as the dominant trees shade them out. But at present this place is a nature snooper's paradise. Most of the trees are still less than ten feet high, and in the summer and fall wildflowers abound —asters, goldenrod, the tall joe-pye weed, and ironweed. This is the only place I can find the beautiful, deep orange butterfly milkweed—a plant that is very attractive to butterflies, hence its common name. We have one of these milkweeds in our garden and it lives up to its reputation.

By now, in midwinter, the flowers are gone. I have come, though, to search for goldenrod—not for its blossoms but for the galls on its stem. Inside these galls is a fat white maggot, or larva, a quarter-inch or less in length, that makes superb ice-fishing bait. (With the recent cold weather, the ice on our pond is almost safe to venture upon.) It is interesting how these galls form. Sometime in summer, a fly lays an egg on the stem of the goldenrod plant. When the egg hatches the larva eats its way in to the center of the stalk. The plant's reaction to this invasion is to form a swelling, or gall, around the larva. This is then home to the maggot through the winter months and if its life cycle isn't interrupted by a hungry fisherman or bird, it will emerge the following spring or summer as an adult banded-wing fly.

I was disappointed as I checked out the galls. (They are about as big around as a quarter and are shaped like a cherry belle radish.) Each one had a hole in it where a bird, maybe a chickadee or nuthatch, had pecked through and fished out the juicy morsel. As I searched for uneaten galls, a downy woodpecker began chirping. I suspect he was the culprit and wanted me out of his favorite dining area.

I left the downy and his domain and went across the road where there was another field of almost solid goldenrod. Here I found lots of galls that hadn't been touched by the birds, and soon my pockets were bulging with the encased larvae, while visions of bluegills danced in my head.

The day had begun overcast, but now as I turned toward home the sky had cleared and the temperature was falling. The snow was turning powdery and the rays of the afternoon sun were already casting long shadows beyond the trees. These shadows appeared blue on the pure whiteness of the snow. E. B. White once wrote, "I am always humbled by the infinite ingenuity of the Lord, who can make a red barn cast a blue shadow." As I neared our farmstead a rough-legged hawk glided silently into the pine tree by the house. Here he will spend the night. It is a comforting thought to me to know that this stately bird from the Arctic sleeps next to our bedroom.

It was a good day. As a friend said recently, "All days are good—some are just better than others."

Sugaring Time

Our sugar camp isn't much; actually, to a serious sugar man it might not pass as a sugar camp at all. A one-horse operation at best, it consists of a leaky 200-gallon pressure water tank converted to a furnace, a metal chimney, and a 2½ × 5-foot pan to fit the makeshift firebox. The apparatus is protected from the weather by a flat roof supported by four posts, a shelter which has on occasion succumbed to the storms of summer. But in that enjoyable time between real winter and plowing, the camp serves us well.

Once the daytime temperature creeps into the thirties and forties from nighttime twenties and the soft, cheerful song of the bluebird drifts across the fields, it's time to tap the maple trees.

Maple syrup was likely one of the luxuries the white settlers took from the forests. Learning how to make it from the eastern Indians, the pioneers soon made the sweetener a staple in their homes. The Indians taught them how to gather the sap in bark buckets using alder or elderberry branches for spouts. Both woods have pithy centers that could be pushed out easily, making excellent spiles, as we now call them. The collected sap was then put into wooden troughs and hot stones were dropped in until the water evaporated leaving the syrup.

Here in Ohio the woodland sugar maples produce sap that averages 2 to 3 percent sugar content, which means it takes around forty gallons to make one gallon of syrup. Of course these figures are averages and can vary from year to year and even from tree to tree. According to Dr. Howard Kriebel, professor in the Forestry Division at the Ohio Agricultural Research and Development Center (OARDC), trees that grow in the open—along fencerows, in yards, or in pasture fields—may have a sap sugar content of 4 to 5 percent. We have noticed, since the trees we tap are in our pasture, that in the first run it sometimes takes only twenty gallons of sap to make a gallon of syrup.

Dr. Kriebel and others at the OARDC have developed what they believe to be a superior sugar maple tree. By taking the best sugar trees from Ohio and New England and experimenting with various grafting methods, they've gotten these trees to produce seeds which are then used to grow seedlings that they hope will have twice the sugar content of our native sugar maples. Unfortunately, it takes at least twenty years under ideal conditions from the time a seedling is planted until it can be tapped. So the jury is still out on their hoped-for Jersey maple tree.

Other winds of change are also blowing through the sugar bush, from plastic tubing and pumps that draw the sap into holding tanks to a newfangled process called reverse osmosis. I don't pretend to understand this sophisticated process, which isn't practical on a small scale, but it involves running the sap water through an expensive machine powered by electricity. The operation is somewhat like the desalinization set-ups used in the Middle East to make sea water potable. Only with maple sap, the cleansed water is thrown away. The sap that remains contains 6 to 10 percent sugar. This process eliminates a considerable amount of boiling. Some people, especially New Englanders, fear that reverse osmosis could do to the maple syrup industry what huge cage layer houses did to the egg market. Nothing of this sort will happen, claims Dr. Mariafranca Morselli of the Maple Resources Laboratory at the University of Vermont. Her argument is that it only helps the maple syrup producers to sell a greater percentage of their product as either Grade A Fancy or Light Amber, the highest grades of maple syrup on the market.

The tools needed for small-scale sugaring aren't expensive or sophisticated. For making your own syrup you'll need several good-sized maple trees, some sort of metal evaporator pan, spiles (available in most hardware stores), a carpenter's brace and a ½-inch (number 8) wood bit, a hammer, and containers to catch the sap. These containers can be anything from one-gallon plastic milk jugs to commercial buckets or sap sacks. If it's a homemade container, a ¾-inch hole must be cut close to the rim so that the bucket can be hung on the spile.

Bore the holes to a depth of three inches about four feet above the ground. Slant the hole slightly downward to allow the sap to run out. Then tap in the spile with the hammer until it fits tightly around the shoulder. This is usually about a half-inch from the catch on the topside of the spile. Now watch the first drops of sap well from the spile bringing with them tiny bits of wood chips; then hang the bucket and listen to the ping, ping, ping of the sweet liquid.

As a rough rule of thumb, do not tap trees under ten inches in diameter. One tap for ten- to fifteen-inch trees, two taps for sixteen- to twenty-inch trees, three taps for twenty- to twenty-five-inch trees, and never more than four taps regardless of how big the tree is. In most years one tap will produce from ten to fifteen gallons of sap.

Once the sap is collected, it should be boiled down as quickly as possible, particularly if the weather is warm. If sap is allowed to ferment, it will taste awful. The container used for evaporating can be anything from an iron kettle to any kind of pan with fairly high sides. I'll not soon forget the time a friend and I visited an acquaintance, a part-time farmer, who was sugaring for the first time. Raised in the city, he was pretty excited about doing things country-style, and he proudly showed us his evaporator. Somewhere he had gotten a stainless steel pan around two feet by four feet with six-inch sides. Since pure stainless steel is a poor conductor of heat, he had to keep a lid on the pan to get the sap boiling. Only a tiny trickle of steam was escaping from one corner. He mentioned that it seemed to take forever for the sap to turn syrupy. When we suggested that removing the lid might help, he insisted he knew what he was doing. Later my friend wryly remarked, "At least his syrup should be sterile."

When the sap begins to thicken, take care not to burn or scorch it. As the sap thickens, it boils at a lower temperature and if not watched carefully it can boil over. Should this happen, a bit of cream dropped in will instantly calm the furious foam. Most of us small operators do not finish the syrup in the evaporating pan but do it on the kitchen stove where it's easier to give close attention.

There are several ways to tell when the sap is finally syrup. The most accurate and scientific way is with a hydrometer. This is a device used to measure specific gravity and consists of a hollow glass tube that floats at a different level as the sap turns to syrup. The sweetness is measured by what is called the "Brix Scale." When hot, the finished syrup is Brix 59, 66 when cold.

There are simpler ways. One is to check with a ladle while "finishing off." If the sap dribbles off the spoon it's not ready; wait for the liquid to "apron" off the ladle. We use a candy thermometer as our gauge. When the syrup reaches 7½ degrees above the boiling point of water, it is finished. Since the boiling point of water varies with elevation and barometric pressure, be sure to determine the appropriate boiling point before adding the 7½ degrees.

In order to remove the niter, also known as saltpeter, the hot syrup must now be filtered through felt. Lining the felt filter with a prefilter will prevent the felt from clogging. An alternate method for removing niter involves letting the syrup rest until the niter settles at the bottom and then pouring the syrup from the top of the settlings. The disadvantage with this method is that the syrup must then be reheated to 180 degrees if the containers are to seal properly.

The syrup is now ready to be used. And few things taste as good as fresh syrup from the first sugaring. Whether on fried corn mush, pancakes, or as a sweetener on cereals, it's hard to surpass. There is, however, more to maple sugaring than just the end product. Louis Bromfield described it beautifully when writing about sugaring at Malabar Farm: "There is a kind of excitement which tinges the whole ceremony of sugar making, for it is the symbol of the breaking up of winter and the coming of spring when the sap rises in the trees and the first faint flush of green follows the streaks of melting snow. The cress begins to grow in the spring run and the chickadees and sparrows to call. After the death of winter it is rebirth, the beginning of hope, a new year with the promise of plenty."

Listing Birds

"Geese!" one of the children shouted excitedly as they came running into the barn. The rest of us almost fell over each other in our haste to leave the milking stable for a look, scaring the cows and even the barn cats who sought safety in the dark corners of the calf pens.

The birds turned out not to be geese but eight tundra swans, caught in an early March snow squall and flying low in search of open water to wait out the storm. We were very pleased, as we had never before seen swans. They were recorded as number 136 on our list of birds seen on or flying over our farm.

Listing birds is a favorite activity for many people interested in the out-of-doors. The more serious bird-watchers keep life lists of birds they have seen. These lists usually consist of birds seen in North America, or they may be more regional, listing the birds of only one state or province or county.

My wife and I began our list for the farm soon after we married and started farming. We thought this would be the logical kind of list to keep as we spend most of our time on our 120 acres and are intimately acquainted with its bird life. If an uncommon or vagrant bird stops for food or rest we are soon aware of its presence, as when a northern phalarope was spotted on our pond one October morning in 1972. This sandpiper-like bird has peculiar feeding habits. The one on the pond was spinning like a top, rapidly picking at insects, mosquito larvae, or whatever was stirred up in the water by its kicking feet. The male of this species is truly hen-pecked: the only maternal duty performed by the brightly colored female is the egg laying. After the female has laid the eggs, the drab-colored male does the incubating and then cares for the young, while she whiles away the Canadian tundra summer with the other females of her kind.

After about 130 species, additions to the list came more slowly. Number 137 was an American bittern, which required some coercing before it could be counted. I was standing on the bridge over Salt Creek when I saw the bittern flying toward me. After a considerable amount of arm waving I convinced the "swamp pumper" to veer to the left and cross a corner of our farm. Numbers 140 and 141 were the common goldeneye and the hooded merganser; both were on the pond in March 1978.

In 1980 the great egret, black tern, and Virginia rail plus some warblers were added. This past year we saw only three new species. A sharp-shinned hawk was spotted as it snatched a house sparrow out of the pine tree and carried its prey beneath a shrub. We watched with binoculars as the little speedster plucked the hapless sparrow and then proceeded to eat it.

Later in the spring, while checking some corn ground on the far end of the farm, I heard a birdcall unlike any I had ever heard before. It sounded like a woodpecker with a severe head cold. A few minutes later I heard the haunting, buglelike call again. I glanced skyward and saw a lone bird the size of a great blue heron flying overhead. But instead of flying with its neck in an S curve as the heron does, this bird flew with its neck extended straight ahead of its body. I used a field guide to verify my assumption that it was indeed a sandhill crane.

Number 165, a bald eagle, the last bird on our farm list, was seen in late September while we were sowing wheat. Through a twenty-power telescope, our oldest son and I watched the huge bird ride the updrafts until it gained more altitude and then disappeared in a straight line to the southwest. Given its size, its upturned wingtips, and maybe above all, its mastery of the air, there was no doubt about its identity. It was an immature eagle and thus lacked the distinctive white head and tail. The white head and tail feathers don't appear until the eagle reaches maturity at four to five years of age. To say the least, we were pretty excited.

As the children got older and more able to identify birds, and with the farm list growing by only several new birds yearly, we started keeping an annual list of birds seen. We begin our new list each New Year's Day and the interest in the faded old list that has slowed to a trickle is suddenly renewed by the new list. We use a 22 × 28-inch poster board on which lines are drawn across and down to provide spaces for 180 species of birds. In front of each name is a space for the date the bird was seen and after each name a space is left for the locality where the bird was sighted. For instance, maybe we visited friends in another state and they showed us some new birds. We'll not soon forget our visit to Andy Schrock's ridge-top farm in Cashton, Wisconsin, where he showed us the dickcissel, which I had never seen before, and the western meadowlark, whose melodious song is hard to surpass. (And of course, we couldn't help but notice their nice Brown Swiss cows grazing on the lush green hillside.)

A 3½-inch margin is left around the edge of the poster where each of us then sketches or draws a bird. This adds a touch of color to the list, which is then put on the wall by the kitchen table. Now the search begins. First, all the feeder visitors are listed. Then we keep our eyes open for the other regular winter residents that don't frequent the feeder. In 1984 we had thirty-four species when January ended. February saw the arrivals of the first robin, red-winged blackbird, and killdeer, but in all, only eight new birds were seen during that month.

In March, with migrating waterfowl stopping at the pond, the list started to grow at a faster rate. By the time the first purple martin arrived on the twenty-sixth, fifty-five species were listed.

April was especially active with the coming of the different kinds of swallows. Pectoral sandpipers and bobolinks were quite common in the fields. Also recorded were the brown thrasher and hermit thrush. The month closed with the upland sandpiper, number 84.

And then May, the month all bird-watchers look forward to. On the first of May we spotted the year's first warbler, the yellow. From then on new birds were seen practically every day until the middle of the month. On the eighteenth we spent the day at Lake Erie and added fifty-seven species to the list. When May came to an end, and with it the end of the spring migration, we had listed 162 different birds.

We saw only a few new ones during the summer. Among them were grasshopper sparrows and a Virginia rail. In September the common nighthawk was seen in the evenings seining the air for insects on its southward journey. During November we saw two species of migrating ducks that we had missed in the spring, the green-winged teal and the northern shoveler, plus the tundra swan. I also saw what I thought was a Carolina wren, but I wasn't certain until it confirmed its identity with a vivacious song. These wrens were common until two successive severe winters in the seventies all but exterminated the delightful little songsters. I hadn't seen one for eight years.

We ended the year with 181 species. The last one was a rough-legged hawk soaring over the farm in early December searching for meadow mice. These hawks are about the size of our common redtail. They nest in the far north and then venture south for the winter.

All members of the family can participate in bird listing. And it can be done while going about everyday work. While our farm list is of birds seen only on the farm, our annual list has no boundaries. We do try for accuracy, though. If we aren't positive of a bird's identity we do not list it. If you live in one of the northern states and one of the children reports a flamingo, there's reason to be doubtful. However, we shouldn't be too skeptical, as quite often the youngster may be right. It happened to me last spring while planting corn.

Our seven-year-old son accompanied me to the field one day and waited on the wagon while I planted a round of corn. As I was nearing the end of the second round, he shouted to me, "Hey, Dad, I saw a scarlet tanager." Since we were a ways from a woods but right alongside a fencerow I was skeptical. "Are you sure it wasn't a cardinal?" I quizzed him. "Yes, I am sure. It had black wings!" he replied firmly. Still somewhat doubtful, I left for another round with the planter and as I again neared the end, suddenly there on the ground in front of the team was a brilliant male scarlet tanager. I guess I'm slow to learn—it was in this same field two weeks before that I had seen the sandhill crane. Birds don't always act or play according to the rules.

A good field guide is essential in order to correctly identify the many different kinds of birds. Two excellent ones are *Birds of North America* by Robbins, Bruun, and Zim, and *A Field Guide to Birds East of the Rockies* by Roger Tory Peterson. There is also a Peterson guide to birds west of the Rockies. Another valuable tool is a good pair of binoculars. These glasses have the ability to turn "many little green birds" on a May morning into distinct, separate species of warblers. Probably the most commonly used are the 7×35 power.

Our interest in birds isn't solely in learning their names so they can be recorded on a list, but rather in learning about the birds, watching their adventures, and studying their ways. Only then does listing have its proper place—I like to think of it as the frosting on the cake.

Living as we do in the country, surrounded by woods and fields and streams, birds are very much a part of our everyday lives. Recording the different kinds we see sharpens our awareness and makes us appreciate even more one of God's most beautiful and varied creations.

Woodpeckers

The downy woodpecker didn't seem to be bothered by the howling wind and blowing snow as it clung to the beef suet on the leeward side of the bird feeder. While the chickadees and juncos were darting in and out of the sunflower feeder, the sparrow-sized woodpecker nonchalantly kept pecking on the high-energy food that would sustain it through another cold winter night.

Hardly a day passes in the wintertime that several of these faithful little woodpeckers or their larger cousins, the hairy woodpeckers, don't visit our suet feeder. The male is distinguished from its mate by a red dot on the top of the head.

The downy, like most other woodpeckers except the yellow-bellied sapsucker, seldom migrates great distances for the winter. If food is available, preferably the larvae of wood-boring insects or beef suet, they remain year-round residents.

Besides the downy and hairy woodpeckers, the red-bellied is a regular visitor for suet, sunflower seeds, and sometimes corn. The name red-bellied seems almost a misnomer for this zebra-backed red-crowned woodpecker. It was so named by Carl Linnaeus in 1758 for the reddish-pinkish tinge on its belly.

The similarly sized redheaded woodpecker visits the corn-crib almost as often as the feeder. It is not common in the winter, but in the summer when the sour cherries ripen, its undulating flight from the woods to the top of the cherry tree is a familiar sight. This flashy black, white, and red woodpecker prefers cherries over grubs any day.

Woodpeckers are uniquely equipped to fish out beetle grubs from deep within a tree. They have long wormlike tongues, which can be extended to astonishing lengths when feeding. The tip of the tongue is hard and barbed, like a miniature straw hook, and bordered with bristles that spear the insects deep inside the wood. The bird then withdraws its tongue along with a tantalizing morsel hooked onto the end.

Woodpeckers' skulls are specially designed so that when repeatedly hammering on wood with their bills they don't pound out their brains. The thick-walled skull and the narrow space between the tough outer membrane of the brain and the brain itself serve as a shock absorber when the bird is pounding away.

Anyone who has been fortunate enough to observe at close range a pileated woodpecker searching for wood grubs can attest to the crow-sized woodpecker's ability as a woodcutter. I was sitting in the woods once when I was startled by a swoosh of wings and a loud cackle as a pileated swooped onto a nearby ash tree. The red-crested bird took a few backward hops down the dead tree, then stopped, cocking his head to one side as if listening. He must have liked what he heard because about then the chips started to fly. In a short time he had whacked out a hole deep enough for his head to disappear into and reappear with a fat grub in his bill. With a jerk of his head and a gulp the grub was gone. The woodpecker chopped another hole and found several more insects, which seemed to satisfy his midmorning appetite. With another swoosh of wings he flew off through the wintery woods.

All woodpeckers are cavity nesters and lay pure white eggs. While the hairy woodpecker and yellow-bellied sapsucker prefer to drill their nesting holes in live trees, almost all the other species prefer dead trees.

As stately American elm trees began to die from the im-

ported Dutch elm disease, they provided not only perfect conditions for morel mushrooms to thrive but also excellent nesting habitat for woodpeckers. Along the edge of our woods is a
huge dead elm that has dozens of woodpecker holes in it. If one
sees a dead elm with no holes, it's bound to be a slippery or red
elm. These trees are too hard for woodpeckers to excavate. We
cut the red elm for firewood and leave the American elm for the
birds.

Most woodpeckers use their nesting burrows only one season (the common flicker is an exception). These cavities are
then used the following year by many other species of birds
such as chickadees, titmice, bluebirds, house wrens, nut-
hatches, great crested flycatchers, and, unfortunately, the
bossy starlings and house sparrows. Wood ducks will use old
pileated woodpecker nests.

Many ornithologists are of the opinion that the lumbering
of mature forests and the removal of dead trees in the bottom-
lands and swampy forests of the Atlantic and Gulf coastal
plains contributed greatly to the decline of America's most
majestic woodpecker, the ivorybill. Few birds generate more
interest in ornithological circles than the large ivorybill. Especially now that there have been confirmed sightings of three
ivorybills in the mountains of eastern Cuba.

The last confirmed sighting of this rare bird in the United
States was in the Singer Tract along Louisiana's Tensas River
back in December 1941. This 128-square-mile tract of mostly
virgin timber was owned by the Singer Sewing Machine Company. In 1937 James Tanner from Cornell University was
awarded a grant by the Audubon Society to make a census of
the ivorybill population. In his three-year search through the
South he found five of the big woodpeckers. All were on the
Singer Tract. Efforts to save a portion of the 82,000-acre property for the ivorybill failed, and it was logged.

In 1731 ivory-billed woodpeckers were abundant along the

seaboard. They were found throughout the Gulf States, as far north as Virginia, and up the Mississippi Valley as far as southern Ohio and Illinois. Mark Catesby wrote that year, "The Bills of these Birds are much valued by the Canada Indians, who made Coronets of 'em for their Princes and great warriors, by fixing them round a Wreath, with their points outward. The Northern Indians having none of these Birds in their cold country, purchase them of the Southern people at the price of two, and sometimes three, Buck-skins a Bill."

While on a flatboat ride down the Ohio and Mississippi rivers in 1821, John James Audubon noted in his journal that the species was quite common. Not until the southern forests were cleared for agriculture and steamboat fuel did the decline of the ivorybill gain momentum; by 1900 the species tottered on the brink of extinction.

The recent Cuban discovery has prompted a renewed effort to find the elusive bird in the United States. If none is found by 1992, the U.S. Fish and Wildlife Service will officially declare it extinct.

There are still some people who believe that ivorybills survive in parts of the South. In fact, a few knowledgeable ornithologists are convinced that ivorybills exist in areas where the shy birds have retreated far from the disturbances of humans. These locations are some of the best-kept secrets of the ornithological world. It is easy to imagine what would happen should the Fish and Wildlife Service or some conservation organization announce that a pair of ivorybills were found in the South. Concern over what would occur was voiced by the curator at the Louisiana State University Museum of Zoology. "If word got out about a confirmed sighting here," he said, "five thousand birders would come down to find it, and a few hundred of them would do anything, including break laws and trespass, to find that bird." Castro's ivorybills are probably safer.

In the past twenty years or so a number of sightings have been reported. Some reports undoubtedly were of pileateds mistaken for ivorybills, but others seem quite convincing. There have even been a few voice recordings and photographs of supposed ivorybills, but for the most part these are shrugged off as hoaxes. The birds have been seen flying across interstate highways, and a five-year search by a team of volunteers in central Florida during the late sixties produced eleven brief sightings.

If there is a remnant population somewhere in the wilds of the Gulf States maybe it's just as well they never are found. That way the ivorybill, with its large size, striking color pattern, and its mystery can live on in our minds. And we can always hope to see one fly across the highway.

Arctic Migrant

Yesterday afternoon, while coming home from Mt. Hope, we saw our first rough-legged hawk of this winter. The big bird was hunting for its supper over a hayfield. Facing into a brisk wind the hawk slowly beat its long wings, yet remained in the same position for perhaps a minute, then it flew a short distance and hovered again, hoping to surprise a meadow mouse that had thrown caution to the wind.

There is something endearing about this gangly raptor from the Far North. For one, the roughleg is the only bird of prey from the Arctic that visits us regularly and the only large hawk we get to see that habitually hovers while hunting. And, also, the roughleg is rather tame for a hawk. Quite often while hauling manure we can pass within fifty feet of a feeding roughleg and it will not fly. At times we can even approach close enough to see the reason for its name—legs feathered down to the toes. Besides, when the roughlegs have arrived, winter can't be far behind, a time when we farmers hope to catch up on little things we kept putting off all summer.

In size, this migrant from the Arctic compares with our common red-tailed hawk, although when seen together, as they hunt over the same field, they are noticeably different. The redtail is stockier and swifter of wing, whereas the roughleg has a longer tail and wings and flies with deeper wing beats. Its floppy flight suggests that of a marsh hawk (northern harrier in official nomenclature) or a short-eared owl.

Seen from below, the wintertime red-tailed hawk looks almost pure white, whereas the rough-legged has a broad band of brown across its belly and dark patches on the wrists of its otherwise white underwings. In some cases the belly will appear blotched or almost completely dark. Likewise, the roughleg's tail is white with a broad black band at the tip. This tail band and the bird's black wrists are good field marks to distinguish the redtail from the roughleg. As a roughleg wheels in flight, its white rump and tail are usually very noticeable.

Most of the roughlegs we see, including the one yesterday, are of the light phase. The much rarer dark phase varies quite a bit in color but can be almost totally black, except for the white underside of its wings. Only once have I seen such a dark-bodied roughleg. The hawk was mouse hunting over our wheat-stubble field, and as it hovered it revealed a dramatic contrast of colors—on the downbeat its long wings looked crow-black and on the upbeat the underwings flashed snow-white. A splendid bird.

The rough-legged hawk is a true friend to the farmer. John and Frank Craighead, in their extensive study of hawks and owls in Michigan, found that 98 percent of the diet of the rough-legged hawk consisted of mice, rats, and shrews. Of these three, 84 percent were meadow mice. Studies have also shown that meadow mice have five to ten litters from April through October, and each litter averages five young. Their numbers peak in October and November. Then the roughlegs arrive and, over the course of the winter, they, along with the redtails, kestrels, owls, and red foxes, reduce the numbers of these small rodents to their lowest ebb by April.

When deep snow gives the mouse the freedom to roam without fear of the hawk, the roughleg will feed on carrion. A few winters ago the boys trapped several hundred muskrats. The carcasses the cats didn't eat were taken to the fields with the manure spreader. Throughout the winter, whenever snow protected the mice, two roughlegs dined on muskrat. Fellow diners included four redtails and scores of crows. (I realize that some bird lovers go about carrion feeding in a big way, leaving out dead cows for their feathered friends. Thus far we haven't ventured beyond muskrats.)

By late March and April the rough-legged hawks are well on their way to northern nesting grounds, where they will nest in the company of other Arctic raptors. In the summer of 1987 biologists near Norton, Alaska, banded eleven young rough-legged hawks. In addition, twenty-nine young peregrine falcons, six golden eagles, and five gyrfalcons were banded in the same vicinity—regal company indeed.

A pair of roughlegs will often build their nest on a rocky ledge high on the face of a cliff. Normally laying three to four white eggs streaked with brown, the female, in years of a high lemming population, will lay as many as seven eggs. After an incubation time of twenty-eight days, the young hatch, usually in early summer. Fed a diet of lemmings and other small rodents, they are ready to fly by September. Soon after fledging, singly or by twos or threes, the hawks begin their southward migration. Staying ahead of the cold, they arrive here in late fall or early winter.

In years past, thousands of these birds were shot during their southward journey by gunners stationed at migration bottlenecks. The trusting birds hadn't learned to fear man and were easy targets for the shooters.

Those who do survive the migration flight find an abundance of meadow mice upon their arrival. Having spent the summer reproducing at a phenomenal rate in hayfields, meadows, and orchards, in the wheat and oat shocks, wherever there was ample food and cover, the mice are now everywhere. Thus the stage is set for another winter when only the craftiest mice will live to see the spring.

With interest we watch the roughleg quarter the field, pause and hover, then plummet to the ground. A hungry mouse provides a meal for a hungry hawk.

Night Hunters

The cottontail cautiously left the safety of the fencerow and began feeding on the ear of corn it had discovered the night before. Too late, it saw the shadow of approaching danger sweeping through the darkness. Its attempt at escape was futile as powerful talons ripped through its soft fur. The stillness of the winter night was shattered by a piercing scream. A hunting red fox paused in midstride, every nerve in his sleek body taut, and listened . . . the "winged tiger" had killed again.

The great horned owl rested briefly, and then with large and powerful wings it carried the unfortunate rabbit to its nest high in a beech tree. Though only late February, the female owl was already incubating two creamy white eggs. Now that her mate had brought her food she wouldn't have to leave the nest to hunt on her own and expose the eggs to the below-freezing temperature.

Of all the wild birds familiar to us, owls are probably the most misunderstood and are surely the least often seen. They are, however, frequently heard during the winter. This is especially true of the great horned owls. On cold moonlit nights in January, when these marauders are already beginning to mate, we hear the deep, resonant six-noted hoot—"whoo! whoo-whoo-whoo! whoo! whoo!"—echoing from almost every woods and woodlot around the farm. There likely are many more great horned owls than we realize. The owner of a game bird farm in Wayne County told me several years ago, if I recall correctly, that he trapped forty-five of these owls in a two-year period. He added, "I didn't expect that there'd be that many great horned owls in the whole county."

Unlike hawks, owls seldom miss their quarry. Perhaps their ability to fly noiselessly accounts for these birds' success as hunters. The soft, saw-toothed outside edge on their primary (wing) feathers reduces the noise of the air passing over the wings and allows them to fly almost as silently as moths. Also unlike hawks, owls do not build their own nests; they simply find an appropriate place to lay their eggs. In this part of the country the great horned owls usually nest in old red-tailed hawk nests. Arthur Cleveland Bent, in his *Life Histories of North American Birds of Prey*, points out that great horned owls and red-tailed hawks are complementary species. Likewise, the barred owl and the red-shouldered hawk share the same habitat, as do the screech owl and the American kestrel (sparrow hawk). The owls are active predators at night, whereas the hawks hunt only during the daytime.

Arthur Bent claims that horned owls seldom nest in the same tract of woods for more than four years. He theorizes that because these owls are such voracious feeders, they exhaust the supply of small game, often within one or two seasons, and have to move to new hunting grounds. But a nest in my neighbor's woods has been in almost continuous use since we discovered it in the mid-fifties. The only year that the owls didn't use the nest was 1973, when a pair of red-tailed hawks repaired the nest and fledged two young in it. The following February two ears again protruded above the nest—the owls had reclaimed ownership and have used it annually since.

I tend to think that in a farming area where there is diversified farming, with hayfields and meadows interspersed with fencerows and woods, there are ample numbers of meadow mice and cottontails available for food, thus enabling owls to remain in an area indefinitely. In areas of little or no farming and in parts of the Midwest where the crops are, as one writer put it, "the corn, soybeans, Florida rotation," Bent's theory is probably correct.

Besides using stick nests, great horned owls occasionally nest in the hollowed-out tops of broken trees. From one to five eggs are laid, with two or three being the usual number. Following an incubation period of twenty-six to thirty-two days, the owlets hatch covered with down. Because the newborn are blind, the parent must lift a young owl's tiny head in her great foot in order to feed it. The nestlings mature slowly and may remain in the nest ten weeks or more before fledging. The young usually have left the nest by June, but they still depend on their parents for food throughout the summer and fall. During this time the young owls, begging their parents for food, shriek loud, harsh, blood-curdling screams. I often hear them in the early mornings of late summer and early autumn, when I'm fetching the cows. Not to be confused with the similar calls of barn owls, these wild screams always come from the direction of the woods.

When the young owls become self-sufficient, they are driven by the adults from the home territory. How far do they go? Dr. Paul Errington, wildlife biologist, writes, "Of thirteen horned owl nestlings personally banded, three were reported shot (this was before the owls were protected by law) within a year or so, all at points thirteen to twenty miles of where banded."

Now that the young owls are proficient and fearless hunters, they have plenty of enemies that cordially despise them, but none of these is really dangerous. Save for man, the owls have very little to fear. Crows and bluejays are their chief enemies. It is often easy to locate a great horned owl by walking through a woods and then waiting for the crows to corner the owl and with their noisy clamor betray its location. Seldom will the owls retaliate by striking one of the crows, although I have seen a harassed owl raise a foot and threaten its tormentors with opened talons. Usually it will wait patiently until dark, and then pluck its enemy from the roost and eat crow.

In addition to the occasional crow, a horned owl will not hesitate to dine on skunk or just about anything else that roams its territory. Studies have shown, however, that 50 to 70 percent of the birds' prey consists of cottontail rabbits; meadow mice supply most of the balance.

Since owls cannot digest hair, bones, or feathers, these substances are formed into balls called pellets and regurgitated. These oblong pellets can be found beneath their roosting trees and nests. By examining the pellets one can fairly accurately determine what the owls are eating. The ones I find around here belong to the great horned owl and usually consist of rabbit and mouse fur, and bones, and, surprisingly often, the reddish bones and hair of fox squirrels.

The great horned owl is the largest owl in North America with ear tufts; the screech owl is the smallest. The screech owl is fairly common around farms. Its quavering call is often heard on spring and summer nights and, like its bigger cousin, the screech owl eats almost anything from mice and birds to insects and fish. On a spring day a few years ago I accompanied some schoolboys on a tour of the Killbuck Marsh Wildlife Area. The manager, John Staab, showed us different points of interest, among them a squirrel box that was occupied by a family of screech owls. There were six nearly grown young in the box, three gray phase and three red. John pointed out that these small owls eat what is most readily available, which at the time happened to be migrating warblers. The bottom of the box was littered with all kinds of warbler feathers. At a different time of the year, their diet may be made up entirely of mice or insects.

On the same trip we were shown a nest of barn owls. These owls used to be common in the eastern United States, but now are rare. As the state purchased the farms that were included in the wildlife area, many of the barns were left standing. Mr. Staab then made nesting boxes for the barn owls which were very successful for a few years. However, in recent years many of the boxes have gone unused. The reason, in my opinion, is that as the fields surrounding the marsh, some of which were pasture and hayfields, were left to grow up in weeds in the name of "habitat improvement," the barn owls simply left the area. Barn owls feed primarily on rats and mice and thus need short-cropped fields in order to see and obtain prey. It is to any farmer's advantage to have a pair of these aptly named "flying rat traps" around for keeping the rodent population in check. These silent-winged birds of the night are beneficial and deserve our protection.

Hunger Moon

We call the month January, for Janus, a Roman god. The Indians called it the "Wolf Moon," and for good reason; it was during this time, when snow blanketed the land and winter was at its bitterest, that hunger drove the wolves to approach the Indian camps, hunting for food.

Nowadays wolves pose no threat, and looking across the frosty, glistening countryside on January's moonlit nights gives one the impression of peace and tranquility. This is hardly the case for many wild creatures, however. Caught in winter's icy grip, they struggle to survive. To them, the full moon of January may more aptly be called the Moon of Hunger. Of course hibernators, such as the groundhog and black bear, aren't affected by the severity of winter. Then too, while many insects die in the fall after laying the eggs that will carry on their kind, surprising numbers stay alive through the winter because they are uniquely prepared. As winter draws near, the glycerol level in the blood of insects climbs rapidly. Because the glycerol acts as an antifreeze and a preservative, the insects can live through subfreezing temperatures.

Some animals, like squirrels and chipmunks, store food for the winter. During the fall they become obsessed with gathering acorns and other nuts and burying them or caching them in hollow trees. In mild winters not all the buried nuts are needed—in this way many mighty oaks have gotten their start.

Chipmunks are remarkably diligent in storing food. Several years ago one of them took up residence beneath my parents' porch and raided their bird feeder to stock up for winter. My parents asked our boys to live-trap the chipmunk and move it to the woods. The boys had no problem catching it with corn for bait. However, instead of taking it to the woods, they decided to keep it in a cage in the house for a while. (Mom was not overly enthusiastic.) Though we still do not understand how it managed, the little raider escaped the cage and for several weeks had free run of the house. All attempts at locating the chipmunk failed.

Finally, one morning when coming in from the chores, we surprised Chippy in the kitchen. With everyone's help we recaptured the little animal and took him to the woods. During those two weeks we had noticed that the chestnuts we kept in a bowl to age and sweeten kept disappearing. But we had no idea what was happening until later in the winter when every flower pot in the house began sprouting chestnut trees.

Many other animals and birds do not store food but have to search daily, or nightly, for nourishment. To understand what is happening one has only to venture outdoors after a snowfall. The experience is almost like reading a book. Not only do the wild creatures tell who they are by their tracks, but they'll also likely reveal what they were up to. During the severe winters of 1976–77 and 1977–78 I spent many enjoyable hours snooping around outdoors "reading the news."

Frequently I'd come upon the tracks of a white-footed mouse, which look like two rows of stitches across a white quilt. The mouse, forced by hunger, ventured from the safety of the woodpile in search of weed seeds. Often the tracks ended in a depression in the snow where a great horned owl had surprised the unsuspecting mouse. The evidence was plain: the impression of an owl's wingtips and several crimson spots on the snow. Many cottontails met the same fate when they left the brushpile to look for corn or the tender bark of young trees. So long as they stayed in the woodpile or in brushpiles or cornstalks, the mice and rabbits were safe from the owls, but these places didn't offer a lot of security from the marauding weasels. It was easy to follow the weasel tracks as they traveled from woodpile to corn shock, performing their ruthless deeds.

In the marshes and along creeks, the weasels' larger cousin, the mink, is also on the prowl. Instead of mice and rabbits, it hunts for muskrats. Once it makes a kill and eats all it can hold, the mink may curl up in the muskrats' house and sleep for a day or two.

I've noticed that gray foxes do the same thing. After killing and feasting on a cottontail, they return to their den and no fresh tracks are to be seen for several days. Unlike the gray fox, the red fox feeds primarily on meadow mice and is out hunting almost every night. In times of deep snow, if the red fox finds these mice hard to come by, it will then hunt for other prey, including cottontails. By following its meandering tracks through woods and across fields many of its habits can be learned.

Sometimes there are surprises. Once I came across a red-fox track in the hayfield by the house. As I followed the track I came to the spot where the fox had used a clump of orchard grass for a scent post. As I leaned down to get a sniff to verify the track-maker's identity, I was startled as a cottontail exploded from its hiding place in the grass, showering snow into my face. The tracks indicated that the rabbit had been there when Reynard passed. I would dare to guess that this cottontail was one of the few that ever smelled like a fox and lived to tell the tale.

During the winter, the raccoon and skunk take several long naps, living off their fat. If a January thaw occurs, they awaken, hunt for food, and then, as the cold returns, take another nap.

One animal that suffers in hard winters is the opossum. Like the coon and skunk, the possum lives on stored fat, but for one reason or another around the middle of winter opossums seem to run out of fuel. They must sally forth then, looking for something to eat. I've seen them fumbling through snow, appearing utterly miserable, their ears, nose, and bare feet bright pink from the cold. These marsupials will eat anything their long nose leads them to, from frozen pokeberries to carrion. Nevertheless, if the cold persists the unfortunate possum usually loses the battle. Their numbers will plummet only to rebound in years of mild winters.

In this part of the country the deer don't endure too many hardships in winter because there is plenty of food available. In the summer and fall they are "munchers," feeding on grasses and legumes, corn, and acorns. With the coming of winter they become browsers, subsisting on buds and twigs. Should an unharvested field of corn be in the area, you can always find deer nearby. In the north country, the whitetails group together in protected cover, from which paths through the snow lead to food. This is called "yarding."

Birds, too, suffer in cold weather, especially those species that have extended their range northwards. Since the cold winters of the late seventies we haven't seen or heard a Carolina wren here on the farm, and it wasn't until the summer of 1985 that a mockingbird returned. When there are many well-stocked feeders, most birds fare pretty well. The bluebirds seem to do all right without handouts, though on occasion we find dead bluebirds in our birdhouses, probably having died of exposure. A friend of mine told me that last winter, when the temperatures dipped to minus 20, he watched nine bluebirds enter one box. No doubt, in numbers there is warmth. I cleaned out a box last spring that had over one-half inch of multiflora rose seeds covering the bottom. Apparently this noxious rose is important to overwintering bluebirds.

We can do a lot for wildlife in severe weather by putting out feed. Nothing beats ear corn for woodland creatures. We scatter ears of corn in brushpiles and briar patches for the rabbits. Here they can eat without fear of owls. I also made a basket out of one-inch chicken wire, which is filled with ear corn for the squirrels. We fastened the basket to a tree, about five feet from the ground, with a rubber tie-down strap. Since the squirrels eat only the hearts of the corn, the rest drops to the ground, where it is in turn enjoyed by the cardinals, bluejays, and titmice.

Winter hangs on as the Hunger Moon draws to a close. Now that winter's midpoint is reached, we take inventory of the feed that is left in the barn. (Maybe the squirrels count their acorns too.) Always hoping to find that at least half is left, I never fail to remember an old farmer's rhyme:

> When January nears its end
> On this advice you can depend:
> Have half your wood and half your hay
> And you'll come safely through to May.

Sassafras

"Sassafras is good for just about anything that ails you, but it is especially good as a spring tonic," my elderly neighbor remarked as he bent over a tub scrubbing freshly dug root of sassafras. "Along about February," he continued, "when you're in the midst of the winter doldrums, a spell of sassafras tea will soon have you fit as a fiddle. It thins the blood, which for some reason thickens over the winter. It's almost like putting lightweight oil in a motor; you start and run slicker."

When the first Europeans arrived in the New World, no plant created more interest or was more closely connected with American exploration than sassafras. In fact, the aromatic tree may have figured directly in the discovery of America. It is said that Columbus sensed the nearness of land by the strong scent of sassafras. And this enabled him to convince his mutinous crew that land was close by.

In the late 1500s, a Spanish physician named Nicolas Monardes wrote a book describing the astonishing variety of medicinal plants arriving in Spain from the Western Hemisphere. The book was later translated into English under the title *Joyfull Newes out of the Newe Founde Worlde*. Dr. Monardes wrote that a tea made from the "woode and roote" of sassafras is used by the Indians in Florida to heal "greevous and variable deseases." The tea also had "merveilous effectes" against the constant agues, or malaria, suffered from "the naughtie meates and drinkyng of the rawe waters, and slepyng in the dewes."

By 1582 sassafras was used in Germany and a few years later throughout Western Europe to treat malaria and many other ailments. Demand for the "ague" tree became so great that ships sailed to America in search of it.

The English found it growing on Martha's Vineyard, dug up the roots, and took them back to England. Thus sassafras became the first commercial export from the New World.

The Indians were using sassafras long before the Europeans reached America's shores. The Iroquois, who lived on the northern fringes of the tree's range, were using it not only in cases of rheumatism and as a diuretic but also as a spring tonic. Later, Indian herbalists even peddled the root bark to their newly arrived white neighbors.

In the north, sassafras grows generally as a shrub, but farther south it grows as a tree, occasionally attaining heights of sixty feet or more and diameters of several feet. Sassafras is unique among trees in that it has three distinctly different shapes of leaves growing on the same tree. Some are oval shaped, while on the same twig others may have one lobe, resembling the thumb on a mitten; still others are divided at the outer end into three lobes.

The greenish yellow, fragrant flowers are borne in clusters and appear with the first unfolding of the leaves. The fruit is oblong, dark blue or black, and about the size of a pea. In pioneer times the soft and light wood was sometimes used for ox yokes; nowadays, if big enough trees can be found, it is used for wagon beams and apple crates.

All parts of the tree are aromatic, though it is the inner bark of the root that makes the finest tea. According to Bob Mohr from Winesburg, who introduced us to the delectable flavor of correctly prepared sassafras tea, roots dug up in January and February will produce the most flavorful tea. The tree or shrub is dormant at this time, and the very best flavor is stored in its root.

I'd hesitate to use roots from trees found along heavily traveled roads because of the possibility of contamination by leaded-gas fumes and herbicides. Some township trustees harbor the notion that roadsides are neglected unless annually doused with a weed and brush killer. It always bothers me to see leaves turn brown before their time, especially on sassafras trees, which are not only appreciated by many people but are the preferred habitat for the beautiful promethea moth. The larvae of this moth feed on the sassafras leaves and then spin and hang their pendulum-shaped cocoons from the twigs of the trees.

We have a favorite fencerow where I dig our year's supply of roots. The necessary tools for digging roots are a five-gallon bucket, a shovel, and a hand axe or hatchet to cut the roots. A small trappers-type hoe is also handy in digging alongside the roots. Lastly, you need a warm day following a thaw, with bluebirds warbling and song sparrows tuning up on their spring song, and you're set for business. Plan to spend a good half-day, as the gathering itself is, I think, a vital part of the "spring tonic."

Any roots up to one and a quarter or even two inches in diameter can be used, though some folks think that young trees and small roots make the best tea. The roots we use are from trees three to five inches in diameter.

Once you get the roots home, they should be scrubbed—a stiff-bristled vegetable brush works fine—and washed with clean water. Following this the roots are placed in a tub of water. Using a dull knife, and with a back-and-forth motion, scrape away the outer bark to reveal the reddish orange inner bark. The bigger and older the root, the more gnarled and difficult it is to clean. After removing the outer bark, rinse the roots again with clean water, and then spread them out on newspapers.

Now comes the most enjoyable part. Using a sharp knife

this time, cut the orange inner bark away from the root in small slices and drop it onto cookie sheets. There's no need to be concerned about slicing off more than the tea part, because the white heartwood of the root is extremely hard and almost impossible to cut into. When the root shavings are spread thinly over the cookie sheets, place them over heat to dry. We put ours on top of the wood stove. Caution should be used to prevent scorching. The delightful essence of drying sassafras as it permeates the house is only one more benefit of the "spring tonic." After six to eight hours or overnight the sassafras should be completely dry and can then be stored in glass jars almost indefinitely. Sassafras prepared in this manner is far superior to the chopped whole root that most herbal supply places offer. The tea made from the whole root leaves a bitter aftertaste.

When brewing the tea, one thing should be kept in mind—a little bit goes a long way. For two quarts of tea only around one tablespoon of dried root is needed or a teaball half-filled. Bring the water to a boil, set it off the heat, then add the root and let it steep for ten to fifteen minutes, or longer if a stronger tea is desired. Oftentimes we refill the teapot with water and brew a second batch with the same roots. Sugar or honey can be added to suit your taste. We think this is the tea of all teas.

In recent years some medical researchers have claimed that safrole, the main ingredient of oil of sassafras, could be harmful if used in excess, so drink in moderation.

Today the many cures of "greevous and variable deseases" attributed to sassafras three hundred years ago are generally discounted. Medicinal purpose aside, we drink the tea for its tantalizing taste, and we still get "merveilous effectes."

Spring

Wings of Spring:
The Canada Goose

Along about March even the most enthusiastic of us outdoor people are beginning to feel the monotony of winter. Only a few new birds have been added to the list since January. The birds that visit the feeder have been with us all winter, and even they are showing signs of restlessness. We strain for signs of spring—anything that gives even a hint that winter is relinquishing its hold. To one of my neighbors spring is the rich aroma of newly turned earth, to another it is the rising and rolling steam from the sugar camp. I got my assurance yesterday—the geese returned. I was pushing down straw for the cows last evening when I heard them arrive. I got out of the barn in time to hear the wind whistle through their set wings as they came honking in to the pond.

Canada geese, like us, can hardly wait for spring. Unlike most other migrants who wait until the weather warms and then travel north rapidly, geese return with the opening of the water. Since spring moves north at around fifteen miles a day, the northward movement of geese might be considered a slow migration.

I like to think that our pair of geese spent the winter months in some far-off place such as the Eastern Shore of Chesapeake Bay or in the bayous of Louisiana, and began moving to the north in early February. Maybe they did, but I suspect that they did not even leave the state because the geese that inhabit our area are likely giant Canadas. Of the ten races or subspecies of Canada geese, the giant Canada is the largest and travels the shortest distance during its migration. The giant Canada goose weighs twelve to fourteen pounds, and mature ganders may reach twenty pounds or more with a wingspread of seventy-five inches. They appear huge when compared with the smaller races. There is probably some intermixing between the common and the giant where their territories overlap. The common Canada goose, which nests in northern Canada around Hudson's Bay and migrates south through the interior and eastern United States, averages around eight pounds. The cackling goose is the smallest of the subspecies, weighing only three to four pounds (about the size of a mallard duck). It nests in Alaska and winters in the western states.

The giant Canada was thought to have become extinct around 1920. Some scholars believe that it never existed and lived only in the minds and legends of old-time gunners who boasted of having shot twenty-pound honkers. However, in 1951 Jean Delacour, working from extensive notes left by earlier naturalists, became convinced it did indeed exist at one time and named it *Branta canadensis maxima*. But even he doubted that it was still around, for several years later he said, "The giant Canada goose appears to be extinct."

Imagine the surprise and consternation of the skeptics when Harold Hanson of the Illinois Natural History Survey announced in 1962 that he had rediscovered the giant Canada goose in, of all places, a city lake in Rochester, Minnesota. A remnant population was also found nesting in almost inaccessible cliffs along the Missouri River between St. Charles and Jefferson City, Missouri. After carefully studying and surveying these flocks and others, Hanson estimated that at least fifty-five thousand of these large wild geese were in existence!

It was from the Minnesota flocks that departments of nat-

ural resources from midwestern states acquired birds to rees-
tablish the honkers throughout their former range. Ohio was
one of these states and has now successfully established size-
able flocks at Crane Creek State Park, Mosquito Reservoir,
and Killdeer Plains. There are also numerous smaller flocks
scattered throughout the state.

A dozen years or so ago we bought two wing-clipped Canada geese. They were supposed to be a pair but both turned out
to be females. When spring came around, a gander came winging in and promptly claimed one of the females. After force-
fully evicting everything, including the mallards, from the
pond, the female made a nest using dried grass and down from
her breast. She then laid five creamy white eggs and incubated
them for close to a month. All this went on while the gander
stood guard, begrudgingly letting us fish at the far end of the
pond. After the downy goslings hatched, the family headed for
the water. The goose led the way with the young, looking like
yellow balls of cotton, following her. Bringing up the rear was
the gander, his stately head held high, ever alert for danger.

It was almost incredible how fast the goslings grew. In several weeks they were the size of leghorn hens. When the young
were about half-grown, the adults began their annual molt.
(For about six weeks during the molt, Canada geese are flightless and must depend on their craftiness for survival.) By the
time we were threshing oats in the latter part of July, the young
were full-winged, the adults' flight feathers had grown back,
and they were flying together as a family. They stayed around
until December, and then left with a flock of migrating geese
that had stopped for a rest.

Geese are among the few birds that stay together as a family
for almost a year. The following March our goose family returned intact. As the nesting season approached, the time
came for the family to break up—what a ruckus followed! I felt

sorry for the young, who seemed bewildered by their parents' sudden aggressiveness. After a while, though, the yearlings gave in and left the area.

Our pair of geese raised a brood each spring for three years, but when the fourth March came, no geese arrived. I had to think of Rachel Carson's *Silent Spring*. Finally, toward the end of the month, the gander came by himself. For days he flew from pond to pond forlornly honking in search of his mate. (The gander was easily recognized by his immense size and by the U.S. Fish and Wildlife band on his leg.) After nearly a week of fruitless searching, he even walked up to our house and stood honking in the front yard, almost as if he wanted us to share in his grief over what befell his family. We mourned with him. A few days later the majestic bird flew out of our lives. To our knowledge we never saw him again.

The past two years another pair has nested here, maybe descendants of our original one. I like to think so. They are almost certainly a young pair, because the gander is much more passive than the old one was. He will tolerate our fishing for bluegill within twenty feet of his mate's nest. The first year five young hatched and all were lost to predators. Last year, again five hatched and two survived to fly. Maybe this year they will have more success.

The local population of these great birds is steadily increasing. Five years ago from forty to sixty geese flocked together and lingered in the neighborhood every autumn. This past fall there were well over two hundred. "What man," wrote Arthur Bent, "is so busy that he will not pause and look upward at the serried ranks of our grandest wild fowl, as their well-known honking notes announce their coming and going, he knows not whence or whither?"

The Horned Lark

If I made a list of favorite songbirds, the horned lark would surely rank near the top. These modest, unobtrusive birds are around every day of the year. Whether in the heat of summer or in the storms of winter, the horned larks are never far away and they're always optimistic about the weather.

Of the seventy-five species of larks worldwide, only the horned lark is native to the United States and Canada. They are birds of the open country. I have never seen a horned lark perch on anything higher above the ground than a rock or broken-down cornstalk. Even though some ornithologists believe that the horned lark may be the most abundant land bird in the world and is common throughout the Northern Hemisphere, the shy bird is almost unknown to many people. Not one of the fifty states named it as the official state bird.

In late January, flocks of winter larks are still here. Two to three hundred are feeding on grains we scatter behind the barn. But sometime in February the large flock will disperse, and only mated pairs will stay. The pairs appear playful as they go hurtling across the fields in the first warm days of late winter. I have often wondered if our nesting birds stay here all year to be joined by their northern kin in winter or if they, too, travel south to return in late February. I have a hunch they're here year-round.

According to the field guides, the northern race of horned larks may appear darker over the back and have more yellow above the eyes than the prairie race, our summer lark. In our flock this winter I've noticed birds that fit the description both of the northern and of the prairie races, with various shades in between.

By March the larks are nesting. The nest is made in an excavated hollow against a clump of grass, the top edge flush with the ground. The female alone builds the nest in two to four days and lines it with fine grasses. What is unique about the nest and, to me, makes it a work of art, is the patio she builds along one side. This doorstep is made of pea-sized pebbles and small shreds of cornstalks. It extends out from the nest about an inch and is maybe two inches wide. All the nests I have found have had the patio along the southeast rim of the nest, toward the morning sun. Scientists are somewhat puzzled by this behavior. My guess is that the patio serves the same purpose as our cement sidewalks. In March, throughout much of the horned lark's range, there are nights when the temperature dips below freezing. When the ground thaws during the daytime the larks, alighting first on the patio, can enter the nest without muddy feet. Anyone who has sown clover seed on a March morning as the ground was thawing knows what a hindrance mud can be—each boot becoming eight inches wide and weighing twenty pounds.

When we're sowing legume seeds on wheat ground, we often find the lark nests. The dropping seeds cause enough disturbance to flush the incubating bird from its nest. The nest we found last year had three eggs, the usual number for early clutches. I mentally marked the location, and as we plowed the next field, I'd occasionally check and admire the beauty of the nest backed against a tuft of wheat, the brownish speckled eggs, and the patio. A week later we got twenty inches of wet snow and the nest was lost.

One nest I found a few years ago might have saved eggs or nestlings in a lesser snowfall. A piece of aluminum measuring approximately three inches by eight inches somehow ended up in the wheatfield, possibly blown in by a storm or hauled out with manure in a previous rotation. The metal was bent in the shape of an inverted V, with the ends stuck into the soil. Beneath this "roof" a horned lark had hollowed out a depression and made its nest with the usual patio out front. When I found this ingenious nest while shocking wheat in July, the young had likely been fledged for several months.

The song of the horned lark has been described as a high-pitched irregular musical twitter. To us it sounds like the distant tinkling of tiny bells. Not loud, but beautiful nevertheless. A familiar sound of the open spaces.

The male is famous for his courtship flight song, which he sings from a height of 250 to 800 feet. Even though I've been around horned larks most of my life I had never seen this display from start to finish until a few springs ago. We were sowing oats and got a notion to finish the field after evening chores. About sundown, after walking behind the grain drill all day, my feet were ready for a ride, so my son said he would sow and I should take the cultipacker. As I reached the top of the hill, I began to feel a pleasant somnolence from the sheer luxury of riding, when suddenly from in front of the team a horned lark took flight. I stopped and watched. The lark flew almost straight up, pausing occasionally, until he was barely visible in the fading light. Then he spread his wings, soared like a hawk, and began singing his delightful courtship song, which to some folks sounds like, "quit, quit, quit, you silly rig and get away." Having sung once, he would flap his wings a few times, soar and repeat the song. After about five minutes of gliding and singing the lark folded his wings and plunged earthward until, when several feet from the ground, he opened his wings and landed at almost the exact spot from which he rose.

I'm reminded of Shelley's poem "To a Skylark":

Hail to thee, blithe spirit!
  Bird thou never wert,
That from heaven, or near it,
  Pourest thy full heart
In profuse strains of unpremeditated art.

Likewise, hymn 47 in the Ausbund, our hymnal, might also re-
fer to Shelley's European skylark, so closely related to our
horned lark in habits and in song:

Die Lerch sich durch die Wolken schwang,
Mit süsser Stimm und Weise.

(The lark wings through the clouds,
With sweet voice and melody.)

When, at the end of winter, this hymn is sung in church, I
think of the horned lark.

Wetland Music

When the winters are long and cold, as this past one was, we often long for the sun and the warmth of spring, and the sounds that accompany it.

The first redwing "o-kee-leeing" from the top of the maple tree; the clamor of northward-winging geese; the warbling song of the bluebirds as they check out the nesting boxes—all are indeed convincing signs that spring is approaching. But the real clincher, in my estimation, is when the spring peepers begin their piping calls. This eagerly awaited event occurs when the daytime temperature gets up to 50 degrees and stays there for three or four days in a row. At first, only a few hardy peepers call, but as the sun warms, they are soon joined by a shrieking chorus.

It seems spring plowing and spring peepers go together. It is usually when we're turning the gently resisting sod that the first shrill cries are heard echoing from a little bog in a neighbor's woods. They mingle well with the sounds of squeaking leather and popping alfalfa roots. The frogs' timing seems to vary over three weeks from year to year. Last year the tiny peepers began their calling on April 2, which was late. Two years ago the first one was heard on March 7, but then cold weather returned and they didn't resume piping until the last day of the month. On the average, though, the peepers quit their hibernation, emerge from the mud, and begin calling around the time of the vernal equinox, or about a week before the first martins arrive.

The spring peeper is in the tree frog family. Its scientific name is *Hyla crucifer*; the crucifer refers to the dark cross on its back. The cross is usually in the form of an X and quite often not too perfect. Barely an inch and a quarter long, the reddish brown frog is rarely found far from water.

For years I listened to the joyous song of spring peepers, yet I had never seen a live one. The shriveled specimen we had in an alcohol-filled jar at school didn't seem to do justice to such an able musician. So one warm April night a friend and I donned hip boots and headed for a nearby marsh, hoping to catch a glimpse of a peeper.

As we waded carefully through the shallow water, around bushes and clumps of weeds, every voice became silent. After we stood motionless for ten minutes or so, a few peepers in the distance began calling again, and soon the whole marsh was reverberating with hundreds of shrill voices. Following the initial hush we could then move around slowly, and with our flashlights we soon found quite a few of the well-camouflaged frogs. They had climbed a few inches out of the water and clung to blades of grass, cattails, or whatever was available.

By inflating the throat sac to the size of a pea (actually the peeper's whole body seems to inflate somewhat), it utters an incredibly shrill "peep." When the weather is warm they "peep" at a rate of once every second. Is it any wonder that to some people a large chorus of peepers, at a distance, sounds like the tinkling of sleigh bells?

The peepers' cry is a mating call and maybe a call of triumph—at least it sounds so to me—at having survived another winter.

Amid the din of peepers, if we listen carefully, other voices can be heard. One belongs to the western chorus frog whose call is a regularly repeated "crreeek" rising in pitch towards the end. The sound can be fairly well imitated by running a thumbnail across the ends of a fine-toothed pocket comb. A low-pitched snore comes from the pickerel frog. This unusual call has little carrying power because it is often uttered while the male is completely submerged. The leopard frog sounds somewhat similar to the pickerel frog, but is louder.

Another frog in the same family as the peeper is the gray tree frog. Its musical trill is usually heard resounding from trees and shrubs throughout late spring and early summer—long after the peepers have ceased their serenading.

Most of us are familiar with the "buloo, blu" croak of the common green frog and the loud, vibrant "ter-rump" or "jug-o-rum" of the big bullfrog, which can grow up to twelve inches long. This is the frog that furnishes the delicacy so enjoyed by many folks—frog legs. A friend once told me he'd never enter a swamp in pursuit of frogs because to him it seemed the peepers were screaming "too deep, too deep" and the bullfrogs were bellowing "better-go-'round, better-go-'round"!

A week or two after the peepers have begun their incessant piping, a voice is heard rising from their midst which is probably the most beautiful of all batrachian sounds: the pure sustained trill of the American toad. It is hard to believe that our common garden toad is such an adept musician. Unlike peepers and other frogs, which are marsh dwellers, toads are dry-land creatures. The most recognizable difference between frogs and toads is that frogs have smooth skin and toads are warty.

It is the male toad that does the singing, supposedly to attract a mate. When a female toad is four years old, she makes a trip to a pond or marsh, usually to the place where she was born, to lay her eggs. Accompanied by her mate, she swims slowly along the edge of the pond leaving a double string of eggs. Once her five to six thousand eggs are produced, she leaves the pond and hops back to the garden or wherever it is that she spent the previous summer.

Female toads seek out a shaded place to spend the daylight

hours. Last summer one stayed half-buried beneath our rhubarb plant, where she remained cool and comfortable even on the warmest days. At night she hopped out and fed on insects in the lawn and garden, snatching them with her tongue which, anchored in the front of her mouth, flicks out faster than the human eye can follow.

A few days after the female toad leaves the pond, tiny tadpoles hatch and drop to the bottom. We often watch the tadpoles as they swarm through clouds of algae along the pond's edge. Here they find food and refuge from their enemies, which are many. Crows, herons, and grackles walk the edge of the water hoping to catch the unwary tadpoles. Should they venture away from the algae into deeper water, the bass and bluegills are always eager to dine on them. Of the many thousands of eggs laid and hatched, only a small number survive to live the lives of adult toads.

When the tadpoles have developed lungs and have grown four legs and lost their tails (the tails are absorbed and used as nourishment), they are ready to leave the water. The frogs will stay close to water and wetlands where, if disturbed, they can take a leap or two and regain safety. The young toads, however, venture far across dry land. Most of us who farm have seen toads in early fall, hardly bigger around than a nickel, in the middle of plowed fields. Many times I have assisted them in their attempts to escape the team and harrow.

The toads have several means of protecting themselves. One is their ability to blend in perfectly with their surroundings; another is the glands around their neck which release a bitter-tasting substance that dogs and other potential enemies find extremely disagreeable.

By October or November when cold weather returns, frogs bury themselves in the silt and mud in the bottom of ponds and marshes. Toads, on the other hand, hibernate by burrowing into the ground or into the compost heap until they're below the frostline. When the sun and rains of March and April arrive, they make their way to the surface, and we are again entertained by a mixed chorus of pipings, trills, and snores from the wetlands.

Woodland Jewels

Years ago, Henry Ward Beecher wrote, "Flowers are the sweetest things that God ever made and forgot to put a soul into." This sentiment rings especially true when the parade of wildflowers gets under way in April. Maybe it's the shortness of their stay that makes us treasure them so much. The woodland flowers have very little time to bloom and form tiny beginnings of next year's flowers before they're shaded out by the emerging leaves of the trees.

I often miss the first flowers of spring, those of the skunk cabbage. Within the spiked hood of this wetland plant appears what we hardly recognize as a flower. Bees, though, diligently seek out skunk cabbage for the golden pollen the flowers so liberally produce.

The first "real" wildflower to appear is coltsfoot. These bright yellow blossoms, which at first glance look like dandelions, often grow along roadsides and woods' edges. They bloom as soon as the spring sun warms the soil. The leaves come later and have the shape and size of a colt's hoof. Coltsfoot, along with many other roadside flowers, is an alien. It was brought to America by the colonists for use in herbal medicine and has marched steadily westward, becoming common in this region only within the past two decades.

When I attended school during the 1950s our teacher, naturalist C. F. Zuercher, offered a new pencil to the pupil who brought in the first flower of each species. One requirement was that we should bring the entire plant with enough soil around the roots so that it could be transplanted. Often we carried a paper towel or a crumpled Dixie cup in our pockets in case we came upon a new find. However, many wildflowers made their debut in the schoolroom gently cradled in a handkerchief.

The spring beauty was usually the first to be brought in by a beaming student whose reward was the first pencil. Not only are these dainty white or pale pink flowers among spring's earliest, but they are also likely to be one of the most common and best known. We have a knoll in our pasture that has been colonized by spring beauties, and when they are in full bloom, the knoll seen from a distance looks almost snow-covered.

Following close behind the spring beauty is the bloodroot, whose delicate white blossoms fold up at night and last only a few days. If its root is broken, it "bleeds" a reddish orange sap, as its name implies. It is said that the Indians used the juice of the bloodroot to make war paint.

Another early spring flower is the large-flowered or white trillium. The name *trillium* means "three-leaves." The leaves, petals, and sepals are in whorls of three. Rarely one is found with four leaves. It thrives in moist woods and its large white flowers turn pinkish as they age. Other members of this group are the red and painted trillium and toadshade or sessile trillium. All three are less common than the white trillium. Try to resist picking these beautiful flowers, as the plant will die if the rootstock starves. Besides, some trilliums, especially the red, also called wakerobin, have an offensive odor.

A sweet-scented wildflower is the downy phlox. This bluish lavender flower smells like lilac and is found growing over a wide area. One spring evening, two years ago, my wife's parents came for a visit. Since it had rained in the afternoon, we decided to walk down to the woods; mushrooms were on our minds. Mushrooms we didn't find, but what we did see was even more pleasing. One small section of woods was literally carpeted with downy phlox and yellow ragwort. As the golden rays of the setting sun filtered through the rain-washed leaves of the trees and splashed across the yellows and blues of the ragwort and phlox, their vivid colors against the dark green of the woods seemed to leap out at us. This natural flower garden, to us, was more beautiful than any human-planted one we had ever seen.

Not all wildflowers are as common as the downy phlox or spring beauty. Some wildflowers that are rare close to our home may be fairly common in other communities—for instance, Dutchman's-breeches or lady's slipper or trailing arbutus.

Unfortunately, many wildflowers bloom when we're busy sowing oats and preparing the ground for corn. During this time our nature snooping is pretty much restricted to our own and several neighboring woods. And while we may on occasion see a rare bird in our backyard, that opportunity just doesn't exist with wildflowers. They are rooted to the ground and move little from year to year, and to get a glimpse of their beauty, we must go to them. Thus I had never found the hepatica. Until two years ago, that is, and what a surprise it was.

A schoolteacher friend, Laura Yoder, asked me to accompany her and her students on a nature walk. Though it was only mid-April—a bit early for the bird migration and even a little early for many wildflowers—I was excited nevertheless, because it gave me an excuse to take a half-day off from work in the field to check on the natural world.

The weather that day was beautiful, sunny and mild. As we all know, the enthusiasm of school children has almost no limits, and soon they were bringing us anything from coltsfoot blossoms to centipedes for identification. With the help of the field guides we had along, we were able to name most of our finds. And then one of the pupils handed me a single flower still attached to its stem. The stem was hairy and the blossom a deep lavender-purple. I could hardly believe it. Hepatica! A writer once said of the lovely hepatica that "the white ends of its stamens [shine] against its deep purple cup like stars in a summer night." We then found on a slope alongside a nearby ravine six or eight of the beautiful plants. Now we know where they are.

For a number of years we had only once seen the Canada lily. Then several years ago while walking home from blackberry picking, we came to a clearing where at least two dozen of the stately plants were blooming. The open woods they were in had been previously pastured and then fenced off for maybe ten years. The following year cattle were again turned in, and the handsome red flowers disappeared as quietly as they had appeared.

The parade of wildflowers is almost endless and many more could be mentioned, like the wood and rue anemones, the toothworts, bluets, wild geranium, trout lily, Jacob's ladder, and jack-in-the-pulpit, also known as Indian turnip.

My neighbor's woods is home to scattered clumps of the latter. As Jack, in early May, stands in his pulpit beneath a green-and-purple-striped sheath, there's often a choir of scarlet tanagers and vireos overhead.

Then too, there are the violets. In the Peterson and Mc-Kenny *Field Guide to Wildflowers* no less than forty-one different violets are listed. In early America violets were used by the herbalists for chest and lung problems. Violets, they said, "specially comforteth the heart." They still do, and that goes for most wildflowers.

A Spring Walk

Last May our youngest daughter, Emily, then eight, and I carefully planned an outing. Her older sisters dropped us off several miles southwest of our farm on their way to Berlin. We then intended to walk the seven or eight miles to Millersburg, catch the evening bus, and ride home. This route took us through what I consider some of the most beautiful woodland country in this part of the county. Besides, we crossed some of the farms of friends, giving me a chance for a short visit. We traveled light. Only one pair of lightweight binoculars, a field guide to wildflowers, a Sears sale catalog to serve as a makeshift plant press, a quart of water, some snacks, and a breadbag for gathering edibles. Since the day started out foggy we waited until the warming sun dissipated the fog. By then the temperature reached the 60s. A perfect day for walking. We had no particular subjects in mind. As Emily said, we just went seeing things.

As we left the road and walked downhill toward the woods, our attention was drawn to things yellow. The lush green pasture we were walking through was splattered profusely with blooming dandelions. From a wild cherry tree several goldfinches took flight, the males handsome in their yellow-and-black coats. Then a brilliant yellow warbler sang his cheerful song from the top of a thorn apple, while from a nearby tangle of blackberries and multiflora roses came a spritely "witchity-witchity-witchity," the song of the common yellowthroat. This black-masked, yellow-breasted songster is a warbler, yet its habits are almost wrenlike, as it flits low through the underbrush.

Nearer to the woods a loud unmusical song burst forth from a patch of briars. It sounded like a brown thrasher or mockingbird, because the singer even mimicked a crow. But as the bird flew from the thicket and perched on a greenbriar cane, we saw, to our surprise, that the mimic was a yellow-breasted chat.

The chat, too, is a member of the warbler family, even though it is bigger than the other members of the clan, and its ways aren't very warblerish. In beauty, though, it belongs to this colorful family so beloved by birders.

Our walk was off to a good start.

After getting a good look at the chat we went on our way. We hadn't gone far when we surprised a woodchuck basking in the sun. We laughed as the startled rodent scrambled through the branches of a fallen tree to dive into the safety of its burrow, which was more than likely connected to the cavernous tunnels of an abandoned coal mine nearby.

While crossing the fence to the woods, Emily spotted two deer. They must have seen us coming, yet the shy animals didn't seem to be greatly alarmed. After a little while the deer seemed to have satisfied their curiosity, and with a wave of their white tails they bid us farewell.

Beneath the canopy of the mature maples and oaks we listened to the songs of the eastern wood pewee, scarlet tanager, and red-eyed vireo, and in the distance, the clear call of a rufous-sided towhee—"chewink! chewink!" The male towhee is a bird of contrasting colors. Sporting an ebony-black head, throat, and back, along with rufous sides almost matching the color of a robin's breast, and a white belly, he is a dashing bird. Towhees nest and feed on the ground. They often are seen scratching in the leaf litter for food, hence their local name, ground robin.

Coming to a long-unused field, we stood in awe, dazzled by

the display of blooming dogwoods. We picked one flower, still wet with dew, which measured over four inches across. The dogwoods weren't the only spectacular thing about the field: there were also bluets. These tiny four-petaled flowers were growing and blooming in such abundance that, at a distance, the field appeared frost-covered. Reversing the binoculars and using them as a magnifying glass, we took a close look at the blue flower with the golden eye. Also called quaker ladies and innocence by some, they are very pretty. As a farmer, I must admit that the neglected field with its clumps of poverty grass bothered me. But what a grand way for a field to be returning to woodland.

Reentering the woods, we followed a ravine down to the bottom and then walked alongside the winding creek. We found a few morel mushrooms and a new flower here in the rich bottomland. The flower was in the orchid family, and the field guide showed it to be a showy orchis. Though the lavender and white flowers weren't as large as the related lady's slipper, we were nevertheless excited at finding one member of this beautiful family of flowers.

We continued along the creek, checking around sycamores for mushrooms and watching the trees for birds, until we came to a place I remembered from some years before to be home to large numbers of wild leeks. Using a stick and our hands we dug out several dozen of the pecan-sized bulbs. The leek is in the onion family, and this early in the spring I consider them a delicacy. Dropping them in the bag with the mushrooms I could almost taste the upcoming meal—fried mushrooms and sliced leeks on a warm piece of freshly buttered bread. After we gathered the leeks, we sat down and ate our snack.

Coming to Martin's Creek, we took off our shoes and waded across rather than going out of our way to cross a bridge. The cool water was refreshing, and before going on we rested until our feet were dry. Walking along an abandoned township road south to the next valley, we found two more flowers we had never seen—spring larkspur and dame's rocket.

After visiting with a friend, we crossed his farm and climbed the next ridge. Reaching the top, we saw an American redstart, which surprisingly was one of the few migrating warblers of the day. The perfect weather that had allowed us to get the oats and corn in ahead of time probably also contributed to the dearth of migrating warblers. With no storms to force the birds down, they overflew this area on their northward journey. At least I hope that is the reason. I fear, though, that the cutting down of the tropical rain forests (the winter home for many warblers) to create ranches that will provide cheap beef for fast-food restaurants in the United States may also be partly responsible for the dearth.

Dropping down the other side of the ridge, we came to a plateau of about an acre, shaded by majestic beeches and maples, that was solid with blooming white trilliums and lavender wild geraniums. Off to the left a Kentucky warbler began his rollicking song. The scene was simply idyllic. At times like this I want to remove my hat to the beauty of the natural world and its Creator. While we sat on a log and admired, I checked my watch. Four thirty. Exactly the time the bus was to leave Millersburg, and we were still several miles away. Emily looked at me, shrugged her shoulders, and said, "Oh, well."

Crossing the deep ravine, we found wild ginger on what was now one of our good friend John Y's farms. Along the edge of one of the fields a loud bird song interrupted our trek. I had heard the song before but couldn't recall its owner. The bird cooperated by revealing himself, and we identified him as a white-eyed vireo. Of all the vireos the white-eyed is the least accomplished songster. He doesn't sound as if he were even related to the warbling vireo.

We were now on "solid ground" again, a shaded lane. Here we heard and saw a rose-breasted grosbeak and an orchard oriole. And though we didn't keep a list of all the birds we saw—it probably wouldn't qualify for a Big Day—we were satisfied.

At the end of the long lane we decided to walk the rest of the way to town on a blacktop road. We soon realized we were back in civilization as NO TRESPASSING signs began appearing on trees and poles. We abided by their wishes. This last mile or two on macadam road tired us more than all the miles through woods and fields.

After a quick sandwich and milkshake, we called a friend and were given a ride home, tired (especially Dad) and happy and accompanied by the aroma of wild leeks.

The Thrushes

I was walking along the woods' edge when my attention was drawn to a number of small olive-green birds flitting through the blackberry tangles. As I came closer to the rather tame birds, I recognized them as golden-crowned kinglets. Then I noticed a larger brownish bird in the thick undergrowth. Since I was carrying a fence stretcher instead of binoculars, I waited for the bird to reveal its identity. I didn't have long to wait.

As it perched on a thorny cane I saw that the back of its head and back were brown and its tail, which it jerked occasionally, reddish. It was a hermit thrush. I was delighted to find one of these migrating thrushes so early, only the second day of April. The "onion" snowstorm on the last day of March brought a sudden stop to these early migrants' northward travels, just as it had to our spring fieldwork.

The hermit thrush is one of the five so-called brown-backed thrushes that migrate through this area in the spring. The others are the wood, the Swainson's, and the gray-cheeked thrushes, and the veery.

Unlike the other four, which migrate deep into the tropics, the hermit thrush winters in the southern states and Mexico and may, though rarely, spend a winter in the north. Two years ago we saw one on our Christmas Bird Count. Understandably, it is the first brown-backed thrush to appear in the spring on its way to its northern nesting grounds. The hermit thrush sings what many consider to be the most beautiful of North American bird songs, a song that is comparable, some say, to that of the European nightingale's. Unfortunately, it seldom, if ever, sings its exquisite song while migrating. A bird of the Canadian zone, nesting southward only at the higher altitudes of the Rockies and Appalachians, its song belongs to those who live in or travel to these places.

Although the hermit is given the tribute of being the most gifted, many of the other thrushes are also accomplished songsters. Maurice Brooks writes in *The Appalachians* about the bird life in the High Cheat Mountains of West Virginia: "But the dusk really belongs to the thrushes. . . . At first most of the birds are well downhill, where wood thrushes will remain. As shadows creep upward, veeries and hermit thrushes seek the light toward the summit. Veeries usually keep to the undergrowth, but hermits like to sing from the highest tip of a spruce. Closest of all in approach . . . are the Swainson's thrushes. They seem reluctant to miss one daylight moment, one ray from the summer sunset. Finally, singing must stop, there are a few sleepy chirps—then silence."

Following soon after the hermit is the wood thrush. This is the only one of the five thrushes that stays to nest and sing locally. It can be distinguished from the hermit by the deepening redness about its head, its brown tail, and by the larger, more numerous spots on its breast.

The veery, on the other hand, is uniformly brown, lacking both the reddish head of the wood and the reddish tail of the hermit.

Though the migration periods of the five thrush species overlap, the Swainson's and the gray-cheeked thrushes are more apt to be seen toward the end of the main spring migration. These two are also the most difficult to tell apart; though classed as brown-backed, both are actually more of a grayish brown. (Hence the Swainson's former name, olive-backed thrush.) The surest way to identify these two is to check for an eye ring. If the bird has a distinct buffy white eye ring, it's a Swainson's. If the eye ring is barely visible, it's a gray-cheeked.

All five species of brown-backed thrushes nest in moist, dense woodlands, but only the wood thrush is a true eastern bird. It rarely ventures very far west of the one hundredth meridian. The gray-cheeked travels the greatest distance in migration: often from southernmost Peru to northeastern Siberia and Alaska.

There are four other species of thrushes in the western United States and Canada and one in the Arctic. Only in rare instances does one of these show up in the East.

The Townsend's solitaire, a thrush of the western mountains, has flycatcher ways, yet its song is typically thrushlike. Its melodious song is said to have a swing to it that goes well with the expanse of mountain heights where it nests.

The varied thrush is also a western songster that sometimes, in winter, shows up at feeders as far east as New England and Virginia. Likewise the northern wheatear, which nests in the Arctic, occasionally strays to the eastern United States in autumn. Its usual winter home is in India and Africa.

The brown-backed thrushes aren't the only thrushes native to the eastern United States and Canada. Two other members of this family are the eastern bluebird and the American robin. Robins and bluebirds don't have the spotted breasts of the woodland thrushes, but their young do. We're all familiar with young spot-breasted robins hopping around the lawn, loudly begging their parents for food. As the young reach adulthood, the spots disappear. Beloved by many people, they have, unlike their shier cousins, become dooryard birds and are considered harbingers of spring. Both birds are able singers.

Our eastern bluebird nests as far west as the foothills of the Rockies. From there on one finds the western and mountain bluebirds, which hardly ever come east of the Great Plains.

It has been said that the gentle eastern bluebird carries the blue of heaven on his back and the rich brown of freshly turned earth on his breast. Even though they are more noticeable during the first warm days of spring as the male seeks a nesting site, the bluebirds are hardy and most likely didn't go very far south for the winter. When spring begins, they return to their summer haunts.

The courtship of the bluebird is as beautiful as the bird itself. The male usually arrives a few days ahead of the female and selects a nesting cavity, if one is available, and then sings his sweetest, most melodious notes until a female arrives. He tries his utmost to convince her to accept him and his chosen summer home. If she accepts, they begin building the nest. The nest is loosely constructed of dried grass and weed stems, and the egg cup is lined with finer grasses and some hair. Both sexes help in making the nest but most of the actual work is done by the female. When the nest is complete, the female lays usually four or five, sometimes six, and very rarely seven, pale blue eggs. After twelve days of incubation, the young birds hatch. Both parents care for and feed them for fifteen to eighteen days, at which time the young are feathered and full-winged and ready to leave the nest.

Worldwide there are 306 species of thrushes. Of all these, I rejoice that three share our farm with us: the robins about the buildings; the bluebirds in the orchards and the fields; and the wood thrushes in the woods.

Last spring we were making hay in our farthest field, and, as sometimes happens, our haying day lasted until dark. As dusk approached, so did a deliberate, sweet, liquid voice—*tee-oh-lee, o-lee-ay, tee-oh-lay* drifted gently from the nearby woods. It was the beautiful flutelike song of the wood thrush, neither exultant like the singing of the red-eyed vireo or the orioles nor as rollicking as the wrens, but peaceful, serene, and spirit-lifting. No wonder John Audubon wrote, "How fervently have I blessed the Being who formed the Wood Thrush, and placed it in these solitary forests."

Swallows

Five out of the six species of swallows common to this region have nested on our farm. These graceful birds spend most of their daylight hours on the wing, seeking flying insects. Skimming low over a pond and dipping their bills into the water, they drink as they fly. They bathe the same way; they skim the water with their bodies, then fly off seemingly refreshed.

The cheerful twittering of the spring's first barn swallow as it comes gliding through the open barn windows is a welcome respite from the muffled sounds of the barn animals wintering in close quarters. Arthur Bent has this to say on the barn swallow:

> Everybody who notices birds at all knows, admires and loves the graceful, friendly barn swallow. The peaceful beauty of the rural scene would lose much of its charm without this delightful feature. But such a charming rural scene is not so common as it used to be. The old-fashioned barn, with its wide-open doors, its lofty haymow, and the open sheds where the farm wagons stood are being replaced by modern structures with tightly closed doors and no open windows through which the birds can enter. Horses are replaced to a large extent by automobiles and tractors; cattle are housed in modern dairy barns; and the open haymow is disappearing. [This was written in 1942.] There is no room for the swallow in modern farming.

The rough-sawn joists that support the loft of our barn are ideally suited for the barn swallows. These swallows, with their long, deeply forked tails and rich brown underparts, will not hesitate to build their mud and straw nests on the supports we have nailed against the joists. They seem to prefer to reuse an old nest; they simply reline them with white feathers, and they're ready to lay their four to five eggs.

Unlike the barn swallows, cliff swallows build their gourd-shaped nests on the outside of the barn beneath the eaves. Last year there were around one thousand pairs of these "mud" swallows nesting on the barns of five farms in our community. The birds, with their orange rumps, buffy foreheads, and square tails, are welcomed by the farmers who consider them an asset. By counting the number of visits the adults make to the nest, researchers have estimated that nine hundred insects are needed for every day the young are in the nest. If these figures are accurate, then these one thousand pairs would destroy close to a million insects daily!

It does, however, take some effort to maintain a colony of cliff swallows. First, suitable habitat is vital—that is, eaves that are tightly enclosed. Cliff swallows will not settle where rats and cats can raid their nests.

Second, their worst enemy, the house sparrow, must be controlled in some way, though such interference poses its own problems. I know of several instances in which these swallows attempted to establish a new colony, and as soon as the first nests were nearly completed the house sparrows began to take over. When the sparrows were eliminated by shooting, the swallows abandoned the site, very likely because of the disturbance created by the shooting. In an established colony, however, the swallows apparently aren't bothered by this method.

Frequently, in the early years of our cliff swallow colony, a hard-driving rain would cause the nests to become waterlogged and drop to the ground. This problem was solved by nailing wooden cleats under the eaves, with about four inches of clearance, to which the swallows could conveniently attach their nests. Five years ago they were running out of space, and so I added a second row of cleats four inches below the first.

Unseasonable weather takes its toll on swallows. In June 1979, we had five days that were cool and rainy. The birds suffered from the cold and lack of food. After the weather cleared and things returned to normal, I noticed that the entrance to a cliff swallow's nest was plugged by one of their dead. We set up a ladder and checked the nest. We were surprised at what we found: eleven dead adult swallows and four eggs. Apparently they had crowded together for warmth, and when the one in the entrance died, they all perished. The cliff and barn swallows are different from the martins in that they lay their eggs as soon as their nests are completed. This enables them to raise two broods. I have found the shells of hatched eggs on the ground beneath the nests as early as mid-May and as late as mid-August.

Swallows are swift, strong flyers. While I'm mowing hay or wheat stubble I enjoy watching them as they turn and dive—sometimes within several feet of my face—for the insects stirred up by the mower. Once, I was mowing on a windy day when what looked like a tree cricket was disturbed by the mower knife and flew downwind, hitting me in the face. I was roused to attention, and my gaze followed its flight. It hadn't traveled ten feet when a cliff swallow came from behind and snatched it out of the air. The timing was perfect.

When we're bringing the cows home from the pasture field, we sometimes see one of the less conspicuous members of the swallow family—the rough-winged swallow. These brownish birds nest in burrows dug into banks. Unlike the bank swallows, which nest in colonies in abandoned gravel and sand pits or in sawdust piles, the roughwings tend to be more solitary, preferring to have their burrows along creek banks.

For a number of years several pairs raised broods in old kingfisher burrows along our creek. I noticed, however, that there always seemed to be more swallows than available nesting sites. I racked my brain, trying to think of something I could use to bore holes for more nesting space. A short while later I was in the local hardware store when I chanced to see a corner fencepost anchor. It occurred to me that this three-foot-long rod with its four-inch auger blade on one end would be perfect for the job.

That spring we drilled four two-foot-deep holes. As we finished the first hole and were leaving, a pair of swallows was already darting about and inspecting the new burrow. Two days later the twig and grass nest was completed and contained one white egg. Three of the four burrows we made were used.

There was one problem the first year: the four-inch opening was too big, and several nests were destroyed, possibly by raccoons. The next year the auger was trimmed down to three inches in diameter. Last summer eleven out of twelve of our "manmade" burrows were used, and all the young swallows were successfully fledged. The twelfth hole was enlarged and used by a pair of belted kingfishers. The roughwings don't follow swallow tradition—they raise one brood and are gone by July.

People maintaining bluebird trails recognize the green-above-and-white-below swallow that nests in tree cavities—the tree swallow. Only occasionally has a pair of these swallows nested in our boxes. Maybe we're fortunate, for they are more aggressive than the gentle bluebirds and thus claim many of the houses. But they, too, are beautiful and beneficial birds, and we have always considered it a privilege to have a pair of tree swallows as tenants in one of our bluebird houses.

There is a saying that one swallow does not make a summer, but here on our farm the swallows are very much a part of our lives during the summertime. Each morning we wake to the rich, gurgling sounds of the purple martins, the largest member of the swallow family. Though maybe not considered musical when compared to the songs of the warbling vireo or the orchard oriole, their cheerful chattering is nevertheless a pleasing sound to listen to on our way to do the barn chores.

Admired and protected by people young and old, the purple martin is probably the most sought-after bird in North America. Even before the first Europeans arrived, the Indians were attracting martins to their villages by hanging hollowed-out gourds from poles or trees. Similar gourds are still used in some of the southern states.

The chirruping warble of the first martin as he alights on the box is one of the highlights of spring. The martin houses are then opened. We have found that by waiting to open the houses until the birds arrive, the starlings and house sparrows are easier to control. Though these gangsters create trouble throughout most of the early spring, they aren't firmly entrenched when the late-nesting martins come. Even though the first birds arrive in late March, no serious thought is given to laying their four to five white eggs until well into May. By then the martins are in such abundance that the sparrows are actually pushed back, and the villainous starlings have likely taken over some hapless woodpecker's nesting cavity.

The martins don't build elaborate nests. Both sexes build the nest with a great deal of vocal effort. The nesting material, I've noticed, varies from year to year. It usually consists of straw, strips of cornstalk, and shreds of bark and grasses. One year many of the nests consisted solely of dried quack grass roots or rhizomes which they picked up from the cultivated fields. Occasionally, a rim of mud is placed around the front of the nest to keep the eggs from rolling out the entrance. And almost all the nests contain a few green leaves from the Chinese elm tree in our yard. I'm not sure why—maybe the leaves help in controlling parasites such as mites and lice.

Heavy parasite infestation causes nestlings to leave the nest prematurely. In other words, they simply can't stand it any longer, and so they jump out before they're ready to fly. Many martin enthusiasts use the insecticide Sevin to control the problem. This insecticide, though, isn't recommended for use during the nesting period. Diatomaceous earth, a natural product, can be used safely and is fairly effective in keeping the mites in check. We usually wait until the birds have departed, then we clean and disinfect the houses. It helps that our houses are made of cedar, which is considered somewhat repellent to mites.

As with other species of swallows, unseasonable weather is probably the cause of more martin casualties than all their enemies combined. Many of us remember when Hurricane Agnes moved up the East Coast in June 1972. We were on the western edge of this massive weather system, and as a result of the counterclockwise winds, we had cold northerly winds and rain for close to ten days. Many martin colonies were devastated, not so much by the cold as by the lack of their essential food—flying insects.

Elmer Gerber, from near Kidron, Ohio, had a large colony at the time of the storm, but the next year not a single pair returned. He scatters egg shells on his driveway, and though martins from a neighboring colony come in to eat them, they will not nest in Elmer's boxes. One would think that after twelve years none of the original birds would still be around and that the succeeding generations would again return to nest, but this has not happened.

We were more fortunate. Our surviving martins, too, left that year before the end of June, but the following spring fourteen pairs returned and have gradually built up until well over a hundred pairs are nesting here this year.

Evidently, many of the mature martins occupy the same nesting cavity year after year. My father recalls that when he was a boy, a male martin with a white primary feather returned to the same compartment for nine consecutive nesting seasons. Upon his return, should another martin be in "his" compartment, a scuffle would ensue and the squatter was evicted.

Martins have long been praised for their habit of eating mosquitoes, but recently some ornithologists have doubted these claims. They theorize that since mosquitoes are nocturnal insects, the diurnal martins couldn't possibly devour them by the thousands as they are said to do. But not all mosquitoes fly only at night. And with the martins and swallows flying overhead, we can sit in the yard during the evening unmolested by mosquitoes.

Some of the other insects that martins eat or feed to their young are ants, wasps, horseflies, robber flies (which prey on honeybees), bugs, beetles, moths, dragonflies, and occasionally bees. The martins' habit of eating an occasional bee engendered the only complaint I have ever heard railed against these gentle birds. Alexander Wilson wrote of a man who hated martins: "This was a close-fisted German, who hated them because 'they eat his peas.' I told him he must certainly be mistaken, as I never knew an instance of martins eating peas; but he replied with coolness, that he had many times seen them himself, 'blaying near the hife and going schnip, schnap,' by which I understood that it was bees that had been the sufferers."

A study was done of the martins' food, and in only five out of two hundred stomachs did honeybees appear and every one of them was a drone. I, too, have seen martins catch bees and carry them to their young. However, this was during adverse weather when more favored fare wasn't available.

Unlike the cliff and barn swallows, the martins raise only one brood of young. By the end of July most of these have fledged and, along with the adults, are already preparing for the journey to their winter home in Brazil. Until recently, it was thought that they wintered in the Amazon rain forests. But there was an article in the May 1984 issue of the *Nature Society News*, telling of the discovery that millions of purple martins spend the winter in huge flocks in São Paulo, Brazil. This region of farms and small towns is similar to many areas in which the martins nest in North America.

Around mid-August the late broods have fledged. Then suddenly they are gone. Sometimes several days go by before we realize the quietness around the buildings.

The summer seems short and I fear we sometimes take these birds for granted. But in the evening following a long day of putting up hay, the air still fragrant with its lingering perfume, it is a pleasure for us to sit in the yard and listen to the incessant sounds of the birds and the laughter of the children. The sun has disappeared over the western horizon—the swallows are almost all in their nests, their soft twittering dies down to an occasional whisper and finally gives way to the night. Now the only sounds are the far-off whinny of a horse and the resonant trill of the gray tree frog. Then thunder rumbles in the distance, the smaller children snuggle closer. The hay is in the barn, so let it rain. As we head for bed I remember the words of Solomon: "The sleep of a labouring man is sweet."

Of Warblers
and Mushrooms

There's an adage that says: "When oak leaves are as big as squirrels' ears, and bracken fern is still curled up like a fiddle-head, it's time to plant corn." If we follow this rule, and if the weather cooperates, the corn will be in the ground on schedule, and with the hectic pace of spring plowing and planting behind us, we now have a week or more to pursue other spring plea-sures.

Few things are more pleasant than being in the woods on a warm May morning. Trillium, jack-in-the-pulpit, wild gera-nium, and numerous other wildflowers are sprouting pro-fusely through the rich humus of decaying leaves. The air is pure and fragrant, filtered by the night's rain. The warm rain also stimulates the "popping" of the most prized of edible fungi: the morel mushroom, or "sponge mushruin," as most local folks call them. This time of year also heralds the ap-proach of the spring warblers. And since the wood warblers are largely nocturnal migrants, a nighttime storm sometimes grounds hundreds of them in an area. Ornithologists are of the opinion that this phenomenon occurs when a pronounced warm weather front moves in from the south, carrying the birds with it, and coming to a stop as it meets a cold front ap-proaching from the northwest. Restrained by the cold front, the birds seek shelter and food while waiting for more favorable winds to continue their northward journey. Such "fallouts" are what every warbler enthusiast hopes to stumble upon.

Nevertheless, even if the weather isn't ideal, it is seldom difficult to find a number of different warblers feeding and flitting through thickets and trees. One of the things that makes the warbler migration so interesting is that many species migrate at nearly the same time. It is not unusual to see flocks made up of a dozen species flashing about a single woodlot in their brilliant plumage.

While a few species, including the pine, yellow-rumped, and orange-crowned, may spend the winter in the United States, almost all the others overwinter in Latin America.

All warblers, except the yellow-rumped, feed solely on insects and their larvae. Thus they tend to migrate at a later date than most other songbirds. After leaving their wintering grounds, the small birds arrive around April 20 in the states bordering the Gulf of Mexico and, traveling north with available insect fare, reach the Great Lakes between the 10th and the 20th of May.

Lake Erie acts as a sort of barrier and causes the warblers to linger along its southern shore before venturing on across to Canada. Many make their first landfall on Point Pelee, the southernmost part of Canada, which juts south into Lake Erie.

John Allen Livingston writes on the bird life of Point Pelee in *The Bird Watcher's America*: "As the warming sun gradually takes effect, the exhilarating sound, thin and hesitant at first, begins to swell in volume and intensity. Soon the length and breadth of the Point is filled with the massed voices of a variety of birds. It is claimed that nowhere—certainly nowhere in Canada—is there such a memorable morning chorus. . . . On a good day better than 100 species of songbirds may be compressed in this small peninsula, many of them in great numbers, all of them to some extent vocal. Point Pelee offers the bird listener a rare opportunity to learn the voices of the many northern-nesting warblers, some of which may not be in full song as they pass farther south. The chorus is over, usually, by 10:00 in the morning."

Our commonest warbler, the yellow, nests across the entire North American continent, from the Gulf Coast to Alaska. Many of the others, however, are transients and for a few days in May we get our only chance to see these beautiful birds wearing their brightest colors. In the fall they travel south again, but by then the adults have molted, replacing their rich spring colors with more somber shades, making them extremely difficult to identify, for amateur birders especially.

There are several species which, if we miss seeing them in the spring, we have to wait twelve months for another chance. These warblers travel an elliptical migration route. In spring the Connecticut warbler, for example, proceeds northwest of the Appalachians through the interior of the continent, and then in the fall returns south along the East Coast. Alexander Wilson discovered this uncommon warbler in Connecticut in 1812 and named it after the state. The blackpoll, Wilson, cerulean, and Cape May also follow this circuitous route. They aren't as rare as the Connecticut and usually can be sighted every year. For three straight years a male Cape May appeared in our apple tree by the kitchen window. Possibly it was the same bird, but then again maybe the Cape Mays have a preference for insects in and around apple blossoms.

If you're new at looking for warblers, here are a few hints that might help you. First of all, do not attempt to locate all the species in your first year. It's virtually impossible. (There are fifty-six species of wood warblers in North America. Around thirty-seven can be seen east of the Mississippi River.) Instead, concentrate on the more easily recognizable birds, such as the yellow and black-throated blue warblers, the American redstart, and the common yellowthroat.

Study your field guide well before venturing into the

woods, and if binoculars are available, use them. As you'll soon discover, getting a feeding warbler into your binoculars' field of view while he's darting around in the top of a fifty-foot tree can be a bit tricky. Try to keep your eyes on the bird while raising your field glasses, then focus on a spot on the tree such as a knot on a limb or a crotch that is close to the bird. Once this object is located, quickly move the binoculars to the bird. Now that you have the warbler in your binoculars, concentrate on its markings—the color of the head and throat, the shape of its bill, the presence or absence of an eye stripe, eye ring, or wing bars. After you're satisfied that you've seen all the field marks, consult the field guide to verify its identity.

As you gain confidence in your ability to identify the birds you can move to tougher species, like the Blackburnian warbler which we almost always find in the tops of mature white oaks. The black-and-white is another easily recognizable species. Like a nuthatch, it creeps along branches and up and down tree trunks in its search for insects. If you hear a rollicking song that sounds like a Carolina wren, it's a Kentucky warbler. They're usually on the ground or in low dense cover.

Although the Kentucky and some other warblers have loud and lively songs, most warbler music is subdued, hardly more than a high-pitched "bee-bzzz." At least, so it sounds to me. Yet a lot of warbler seekers have learned the songs of each species and in this way locate many birds.

Unless you live in Mio, Michigan, don't hold your breath waiting for a Kirtland's warbler. This endangered bird's nesting area is restricted to a small portion of Michigan's Lower Peninsula and there only in young stands of jack pines. The present population is estimated at fewer than five hundred birds. They are very rarely seen during migration.

The Bachman's warbler is even closer to extinction. It is thought that possibly as few as several dozen of these birds survive, and these exist in the vicinity of South Carolina's I' On Swamp.

Even though these two species are in trouble, we can take comfort in knowing that the majority of warblers are thriving or at least holding their own and are ours to behold if we take the time to look. Sometimes unexpected rewards go along with warbler watching.

I luckily chanced upon one quite a few years ago when I went to fetch the horses from the pasture field. Since it was a splendid morning I took the long way, which was through the woods, for the same reason that the bear went over the mountain—to see what I could see. I soon spotted a Canada warbler as it was moving through some brambles. This beautiful warbler has a bright yellow breast with a black necklace across it and is most often seen toward the end of the migration. I followed it for quite a while as it foraged through the undergrowth. As it entered a thick tangle, I got down on my hands and knees to get a better look, when suddenly my attention was diverted from the warbler to several big yellow morel mushrooms. Blending in so well with the forest litter, I'm sure I would have missed them if I hadn't been on my knees. After picking a hatful I left the rest; since it was late in the season, many were beyond their peak of freshness.

Mushrooms are considered members of the plant kingdom, though they differ from most plants in that they lack chlorophyll and must rely on decaying matter for nourishment. They reproduce by the spreading of spores. Most spores are so tiny that they can only be seen with a microscope. A single mushroom may release millions of these spores. Given the right conditions—not yet fully understood—the spores that germinate develop through a complex process and eventually appear above the ground as a mushroom.

In the wild, the morels grow in a variety of places. (The two kinds avidly sought around here are the yellow morel and the half-free morel. This half-free morel appears seven to ten days earlier than the regular yellow.) Probably the best place to look for the "sponge" is around dead elm trees. A friend of mine whom I consider an expert in finding morels told me, "I look for elm trees where the bark is just beginning to slip, which is a year or two after they have died. I prefer the American elm over the red [slippery] elm. But, as in all cases, there are exceptions. I've found mushrooms beneath elms that were dead for five years or more, and some 'right-looking' elms never produce." Other popular hunting spots are around old apple, ash, and tulip poplar trees. Last year the best finds were around sycamore trees.

A discussion of mushrooms would hardly be complete without mentioning the different opinions on their rate of growth. Mycologists tend to think that morels reach their full size within a short period of time. Others insist that they "pop" while one's back is turned. Then there are those who claim that morels grow over a period of days. An experience I had would support this last view.

The spring following my mushroom-find I regularly checked my prime spot. I was disappointed, however, to find the small gray morels instead of the nice yellow ones. Since the weather was cool and dry, I decided to leave them to see if they would "grow." The following week warm weather moved in and along with it several thundershowers. Upon checking the mushrooms a few days after the rain (I realize I'm telling this at the risk of my credibility), they had grown considerably. Several days later I picked a mess of what were now yellow morels. The biggest one had grown in this period from a two-inch gray to a nine-and-a-half-inch yellow morel!

I really thought I was onto something. The next spring I again closely watched the mushrooms, but could see no noticeable growth. In the years since, I observed some increase in

size, but it was never as dramatic as that first year. The exper-
iment came to an abrupt end two years ago, when, upon returning to check "my" mushrooms, I found nothing but
broken-off stems. Someone else had discovered my secret
place.

My conclusion is that if the weather conditions are right, the
morel mushroom will continue to grow over a span of days.
And could it be possible that the gray morel is only an immature yellow morel?

As there are likely many more mushroom seekers than there
are warbler watchers, I'd like to offer a suggestion to the mush-
roomers: the next time you go gathering, slip a field guide on
birds and a pair of binoculars into your mushroom sack and
discover what you've been missing.

Summer

Flying Scavengers

As we hurried through the early-morning June woods we were entertained by the voices of nesting birds: the scarlet tanager, the distant trill of a wood thrush, and the incessant singing of a red-eyed vireo, which seemed to be following us. Closer to the ridge, the loud, vivacious song of a Kentucky warbler burst forth.

The bird we were especially looking for that morning is not a musician, though its flight wins our admiration. A friend, Kenny Gerber, had discovered the nest of a pair of turkey vultures (commonly called buzzards by country people) in the vicinity of Winesburg and was taking us along to share his find.

As we approached some rocks that looked almost as big as barns, a vulture took flight from the base of one. Our guide kept a wary eye on the black form circling above the trees, as he was well aware that the big scavengers have the undainty habit of sometimes throwing up breakfast or yesterday's supper at uninvited guests. Nothing rained down on us, however, as we crept up to a cavelike opening beneath one of the monstrous boulders.

Using flashlights we soon saw the two young vultures. They scurried to the back of the cave, stamped their feet, and hissed loudly at our intrusion. While already as big as leghorn hens, the two were still completely covered with white down except for tiny black spots on the wings where their flight feathers were emerging. Their heads were bare and black. While no show winners for looks, they were already well equipped for their role in life as eaters of carrion.

We guessed the young to be around thirty-five to forty days old; they would need care for another forty days or so before they would fly away from their rocky home. Once aloft, the young vultures with their six-foot wingspread become masters of the air. On sunny days they can soar for miles with only an occasional slow flap of the wings. As the young birds mature, their black heads turn red like the heads of their parents.

Unlike its cousins, the black vulture and California condor, which find their food by sight, the turkey vulture depends also on a well-developed sense of smell to find its prey. The big birds aren't particularly choosy about what they eat, just so long as it's not moving. Anything will do from fresh to putrid, and this can include snakes, turtles, woodchucks, raccoons, skunks, cats, and pigs. We often see them sitting nonchalantly on a roadside, feasting on a traffic-killed cottontail or opossum. Sometimes three or four vultures are at one carcass, and while one eats, the others patiently await their turn.

The turkey vulture has a penchant for wandering; it ranges over most of the United States and southern Canada, and all the way south to Cape Horn. On the other hand, the black vulture seldom soars north of an east-west line that runs from Maryland through southeastern Kansas to southern Arizona.

The black vulture, with its short square tail and shorter, wider wings, seems stockier than its red-headed relative. In flight it can be distinguished from the turkey vulture by the light patches near the tips of its wings. Black vultures have the habit of hanging around city dumps, on the lookout for discarded goodies, and sewers, where a well-decomposed carp might be found. They will also sometimes snatch baby herons from their nesting colonies.

The habits of the California condor are more like the turkey vulture's; there is no record of the condor ever attacking a living animal. This record won't change in the near future because the last free-flying wild condor, a male, was live-trapped in February 1987. His mate was captured in the fall of 1986, and now the pair has successfully raised young in captivity.

A lot of controversy has centered on the condor, with the different wildlife agencies at odds over the best method of saving the almost extinct bird. There are now fewer than thirty condors surviving, all in captivity.

The condor, with a wingspan of up to nine and a half feet, is the largest of any North American land bird. It used to range from British Columbia through Oregon to Nevada, and into Utah, Arizona, and California. For the last fifty years, from twenty to thirty of these vultures survived in a two-hundred-mile-long area of rugged mountain country in southern California. There in remote regions of untamed wilderness, the condors had freedom from advancing civilization for many years.

But gradually the encroachment of man forced the great bird to the brink of extinction. Shooting took the greatest toll on condors. (What is it in human nature that makes so many of us want to kill large birds?) Feeding on the carcasses of poisoned coyotes also killed many of the birds, and the loss of cattle ranches (where the condors fed on dead stock) contributed to their decline.

Whether or not the condors can be reintroduced into the wild remains to be seen. What worked so well in restocking the endangered peregrine falcon may be more difficult with the condor, since it takes a condor five to seven years to become fully adult and think about raising a family. Moreover, in the wild the female lays only a single egg every other year. After an incubation period of over fifty days, the chick hatches, and if all goes well, it will be another seven months before it can fly any great distance. At the end of the young condor's first year it is soaring and hunting for prey on its own, but its parents may still continue feeding it into its second summer.

It would be sad if the condor should be lost to the rugged and mountainous West for all time.

Magnificent fliers, vultures are at their best in the air. Yesterday while planting corn, I watched as a crow harassed a turkey vulture. Maybe the crow felt its nearby nest was threatened by the big bird or maybe it was just being ornery. Anyway, while the vulture soared in wide circles and even flapped its wings to gain altitude, the crow struggled to get above and behind its imagined enemy. When at last the crow got to where it had the upper hand, it folded its wings to a sharp angle and dive-bombed the vulture. The normally slow vulture, too, dropped into a dive and, by turning this way then that, with surprising agility it evaded the attacker.

The turkey vultures move south for the winter, and their return in late winter is almost as famous as that of the swallows at San Juan Capistrano. At least in the town of Hinckley, Ohio. Every March 17 or thereabout, the residents of this little hamlet proclaim Buzzard Day. This is to celebrate the return of the turkey vultures to a roost near the town. Lore has it that the buzzards started flocking to Hinckley following the Great Hinckley Hunt in Medina County in December 1818. In this hunt, a gang of men slaughtered twenty-one bears, seventeen wolves, three hundred deer, and hundreds of smaller animals that were thought to be threatening the farm crops and livestock.

Whether this is true or not, I don't know. Nevertheless, we did see our first turkey vulture of the year on March 16. And he was headed north—toward Hinckley.

Bats

We had just brought the cows into the milking stable one evening, when suddenly a birdlike creature took flight and silently zigzagged around posts and partitions. One of the girls screamed, "A bat!" Several cats quickly scrambled up onto stanchions hoping to snatch the flying morsel. In the excitement someone stepped on the tomcat, and his yowl added to the din. The bat, bewildered by the lantern light and the commotion, finally alighted on an overhead joist and scurried into a crack where two beams overlapped. Peace and tranquility returned to the stable.

Bats have the worst image of any creature in the natural world, with the possible exception of the snake. This is especially true in Western society. Bats are considered to be dirty, to be carriers of rabies, to live in dark, dank attics and caves, to get tangled in one's hair. Then too, bats are often associated with wickedness. The Evil One is often depicted with the wings of a bat.

Bats also figure prominently in folklore, superstition, and sorcery. For the Chinese, they have long been symbols of happiness. In Austria there was a belief that if one carried the left eye of a bat on his person, he would be invisible. And ancient medical concoctions often contained parts of bats: an ointment made of "frankincense, lizards' blood, and bats' blood in equal parts" was used to cure trachoma, an eye disease. Likewise, a blend of "bats' heads pounded and mixed with honey" was a remedy for poor eyesight.

If one has abnormal things aflutter in the cranium, he is said to be "batty" or else to have "bats in the belfry."

But despite the bad things said about bats and regardless of whether we like them or not, they are fascinating and useful creatures. And they are the only mammals that can fly. (Flying squirrels are gliders, not true flyers.) The Papago Indians in the Southwest use guano (droppings) from desert bats, gathered from churches and mountain caves, to fertilize their fields.

Many misconceptions surround our perception of bats. For one, they are not blind. They have eyes and can see to varying degrees. What they lack in sight is made up for by their keen hearing. Studies done in Sweden on captive animals showed that a bat could hear a fly cleaning its wings or rubbing its legs together. The bat would then dart in that direction and snap up the fly.

Scientists call the bat's amazing ability to use echoes of its own voice to locate food and obstacles echolocation. The bat accomplishes this by emitting intensely loud high-frequency bursts of sound and then interpreting the echoes. In this way the bat can judge the distance, direction, and movement of insect prey, and the nature of nearby objects that reflect sound. Thus, if you hang a string across the opening of a building where bats leave and enter, they will never fly into the string.

Bats are widely distributed throughout the temperate and tropical regions of the world. Around nine hundred species are recognized, by far the greatest number of which live in the tropics. There are tropical bats with faces resembling those of horses, dogs, pigs, and rabbits, and sporting common names like tube-nosed, plain-nosed, leaf-nosed, and long-nosed bats. There are bulldog, mustache, slit-faced, mouse-tailed, funnel-eared, thumbless, and vampire bats.

Many of the tropical bats feed on fruit, pollen, and nectar. These bats hunt by sight and smell instead of sonar. The giant fruit-eating flying foxes of the Old World weigh two to three pounds and have wings stretching to six feet.

The vampire bat of Central and South America is small in comparison to the flying foxes, having only a five-inch wingspan. They feed at night on the blood of living animals. Vampires use echolocation to find their prey. Landing near the sleeping victim, they crawl aboard and use their razor-sharp incisor teeth to make a quick gash in the skin. Their saliva contains an anticoagulant to keep the blood from clotting. Once the incision is made, the vampire drinks its fill and then flies away. Common vampire bats prefer cattle and other domestic animals and only occasionally attack humans. When they do, it is usually the body parts protruding from under the covers— toes, forearms, and nose. A single vampire will consume almost five gallons of blood a year.

The bats found in the United States and Canada don't eat fruit or drink blood. They feed only on insects. Interestingly, bats drink water as purple martins do. Skimming over the water, they scoop up a drink with their lower jaw.

The bat seen by most of us on warm summer evenings darting this way then that way, snatching flying insects, is the little brown bat. Weighing but a quarter of an ounce, it is common around farm buildings and villages where it finds hideaways in cracks in beams, enclosed cornices, and attics. In late spring the female gives birth to a single offspring, rarely to twins. The young grow rapidly and are able to fly when about three weeks old. When they are a month old they leave the home shelter and start hunting insects on their own.

Banding studies suggest that sometime in September many of the little brown bats leave their summer haunts and congregate in caves by the thousands where, insulated from the cold, they will hibernate through the winter. The bats in Ohio and Indiana are thought to overwinter in Kentucky caves.

Another species in our area is the red bat. Not nearly so

common as the little brown, these pretty bats spend the daylight hours hanging in the foliage of trees. We found one while picking blackberries the other summer. I was working my way around the edge of the berry patch, picking the luscious fruits, when all at once I was nose to face with a bat. It was hanging by one foot from the stem of an ash leaf. The bat was orange-brown in color. (My wife called it burnt sienna.) Very beautiful. While we were admiring it, the bat seemed to be unaware of our presence. Then, without warning, it took wing and swiftly disappeared.

Bats are in fact clean and interesting creatures worthy of our protection, even if we may not necessarily "love" them. A word of caution though: they will sometimes bite when handled, but what untamed wild animal won't? Bats are no more likely to be carriers of rabies than a fox or skunk, and they are much too clever to become entangled in anyone's hair.

Hayland Birds

I was making the backcut along the edge of the hayfield with the mower when the female bobolink flew out from in front of the cutter bar. Quickly stopping the team, I soon located the nest with its five newly hatched young. Using the cut hay, I built a flimsy canopy over the nest with hopes of saving it. The adult bobolinks accepted the makeshift cover and continued feeding the brood. But as I feared, my efforts to spare the nest also made it conspicuous to predators. Several days later the young birds disappeared.

Besides bobolinks, quite a few other species of birds nest in the tall grasses of hayfields. These include the eastern and western meadowlarks, horned larks, red-winged blackbirds, savannah, vesper, and grasshopper sparrows, mallard ducks, ring-necked pheasants, and upland sandpipers.

Most of these birds were native to the tall-grass prairie. As the eastern woodlands were cleared for farming by the early settlers, the birds moved east, adopting hayfields and meadows since these closely resembled their native habitat. (Similarly, some woodland birds, such as the robin, moved west as shelterbelts were planted by the homesteaders.)

As farming practices change, the survival of some of these species is directly affected. In the last thirty years, when many livestock farms converted to cash grain farming, thousands of acres of hayfields and meadows disappeared under the plow. Even on livestock farms changes have occurred. Mixed hayfields are declining in favor of pure stands of alfalfa without interseeded grasses, which the experts advise to cut first in the bud stage, and every thirty-five to forty days thereafter. This process effectively eliminates many nesting attempts. Fortunately, most grassland birds dislike these monocultural hayfields for nesting because they are biological deserts except for a bunch of gnawing and biting insects.

Likewise, the advent of the mower-conditioner has also made life hazardous for field-nesting birds. With the teeth of the reel only inches from the sickle that sweeps the cut hay back to the crusher, practically every incubating hen mallard and hen pheasant, every newly fledged bobolink and meadowlark clinging to the stems of hay in that field will end up a mass of mangled flesh and scattered feathers.

Is it any wonder that the bobolink population is declining in parts of the eastern United States? Almost every spring people drive the fifteen miles from Wooster to our farm to see and listen to the handsome black-and-white male bobolink as he flight-sings across the hayfields. We like to have at least one field of mixed hay for the horses and heifers and the birds. In the early spring we seed equal amounts of clover and alfalfa on the wheat ground, which had timothy seeded along with the wheat the previous fall. If all goes well, this will turn into a nice cover of mixed hay with a sprinkling of daisy fleabane, yellow rocket, and a few other tall weeds for the grassland birds to cling to, swing in the breeze, and proclaim for all to hear that spring is a grand time of the year. We then wait until last to cut this hay, which usually, depending upon the weather, is harvested in the latter part of June. In most cases, this allows the bobolinks and the other birds of the hayfield to safely fledge their first broods.

Despite the hazards, some grassland birds are prospering. The red-winged blackbird, for example, seems to be increasing or at least holding its own. The male, with his flashy, scarlet epaulets, stakes out his territory in the hayfield, and if the nest is destroyed, he and his mate will move to the oats or wheatfield. If they're disturbed there by the binder, they'll likely relocate in the orchard or pasture field. The bobolink, by contrast, usually does not attempt renesting if the first nest is destroyed.

The horned larks are also quite successful, partly because they nest so early, often in late February and March. Occasionally their nests are destroyed while we're plowing sod, but they will renest. By the time haying season arrives, their second brood has already left the nest.

One spring several years ago I had a good opportunity to observe the nesting sequence of a pair of horned larks. On a frosty morning I was sowing legume seed on the wheatfield when I came upon a freshly hollowed-out "cup" in the soil between two wheat plants. The ground was slightly frozen but the nest cup was fresh, and since it was so early in the spring I knew it was the work of a horned lark. I sort of "marked" the location by lining up with a clump of winter-killed volunteer oats and a small rock. By the next day the nest was already lined with fine grasses and the "patio" of small pebbles and clods along the one side of the nest was also completed. The following day one egg was in the nest, and then on the fifth day the clutch of three eggs was completed. (They lay three to five eggs, with four the usual number.) On the 23rd day after finding the excavated "cup," the young were fully feathered and ready to leave the nest. During this period of time the wheat had grown from three to four inches high to over a foot and provided excellent cover for the nest and its occupants.

The distinctly American meadowlark is found nowhere else in the world. Though it is classified as one of the blackbird family, its ways are very much like those of the lark. Like the bobolink, it sings its courtship song while in flight or from the top of a fencepost. This spring, one has been using the top of the maple tree in our yard as a perch from which to whistle his clear, distinct, "spring of the year is here" song. Our eastern meadowlark sings a beautiful song; nevertheless, his cousin the western meadowlark is an even more adept musician. We rarely have the western this far east. When one does show up, word usually gets around as to its whereabouts. I vividly remember the first western meadowlark we heard. Friends of ours from the northern part of the community attended church not too far from here one early June Sunday in the late seventies. One of them is a minister, and, while upstairs in the "Abrot," the church's council room, he heard the bubbling, flutelike notes of a western meadowlark drifting in through the open window. On their way home in the evening, they stopped and told us about this western visitor in the neighborhood. The next morning right after chores we hitched up the buggy horse and went over to where they had heard the lark. We heard him singing even before spotting him perched on a telephone wire. And what a song! It was so unlike the eastern meadowlark's song that I couldn't associate the two as being closely related. It is easy to understand why the western meadowlark, with a song so wild and free, is the state bird of six western states.

Meadowlarks adjust quite well to agricultural changes. If their loosely built, domed nest of grass is destroyed during hay making, they will renest, oftentimes in a nearby pasture or headland.

The sparrows, too, seem to adapt fairly well, although in the last five years I've noticed that the savannah sparrows are increasing whereas the vesper sparrows are on the decrease. I used to be able to walk to the back part of the farm and hear three or four male vesper sparrows singing their lovely evening songs. This year, I haven't heard any. Maybe the savannah is the dominant sparrow, and as they move in the vesper sparrow leaves.

Unlike the hen pheasant and mallard duck, who will not

leave their nest until struck by the sickle bar, the adult upland sandpiper seldom is killed or injured by a mowing machine. These once-abundant birds are now uncommon in Ohio and, to my knowledge, haven't recently nested on our farm. A pair or two do nest about a mile south of us and include our fields in their visits. Larger than a killdeer, they have the unique habit of holding their wings elevated for a little while upon alighting in a field or on a fence post. High overhead on summer evenings we hear their beautiful, long-drawn-out "quail-ee-e-e-e-e" whistled call. They are already preparing for their long journey to the pampas of Argentina.

By threshing time the bobolinks are assembling into flocks and beginning their travels south to join the upland sandpipers in Argentina where they will then pass our winter in the austral summer. When they return to our hayfields next year to join the other hayland birds, they will have traveled twelve thousand miles and will again serenade us with their cheerful, rollicking song.

In Praise
of Fencerows

Dividing our farm from the farm east of us is a fence; or, perhaps I should say, the remnant of a woven-wire fence held up by a tangle of blackberries, raspberries, wild cherry trees, and a myriad of "weeds." This fencerow is unkempt and neglected, but it abounds with wild things. This ribbon of life exists by mutual agreement between my neighbor and myself.

Even though the fencerow abounds with activity throughout the year, the apex of its life occurs in mid- to late summer with the ripening of the blackberries and wild cherries and the blooming of the goldenrod. Their abundance invites the greatest diversity of creatures, from the colorful locust borer beetles and monarch butterflies on the goldenrod to the late-nesting goldfinches on the brambles, and the many birds and mammals feeding on the berries and cherries.

Brushy fencerows are in a sense a gift from man to nature—at least if, after the posts are dug in and the fence stapled to the posts, nature is given some free rein. Birds sitting on the fence and posts will pass undigested seeds in their droppings. Some of these seeds of blackberry, wild cherry, elderberry, bittersweet, sassafras, mulberry, and unfortunately, in some areas, multiflora rose, will take root in the loose soil around the posts and later in soil dug up by woodchucks. Chipmunks scurrying along the fence will bring and bury acorns and hickory nuts, while the wind will deliver dandelion, milkweed, and thistle seeds—all ingredients for a healthy fencerow.

In the northeast corner of the field that borders the fencerow is a rock pile along with a few broken pieces of plowshares and cultivator points. Next to the rocks are some shoots of serviceberry (or Juneberry), sprouts of a tree likely planted by a bird maybe a century ago.

This serviceberry brings back memories of my boyhood and the neighbor who used to own and till the next farm. He was a farmer of the old school, intelligent, interesting and full of wisdom, and suspicious of all the newfangled innovations in agriculture. For years he farmed with a Fordson tractor and a team, then finally went to a two-plow Ferguson tractor. Yet the tractor never really speeded up his life. He always had time to stop whatever work he was doing in his fields for a visit with us beneath the serviceberry, a tree he loved, for it was the first to bloom in the spring.

One year, when he was in his seventies, he and his wife were persuaded to visit relatives in Florida, possibly to stay for the duration of the winter. They had never taken a "vacation" away from the farm and, I suppose, had never really desired one. Within a week they were home. There under the serviceberry he told us, thumbs hooked into the bib of his overalls, that Florida was the poorest place he ever saw. "Why, I saw the skinniest rabbits you can ever imagine," and then, with a look of disgust on his face, he added, "and the people walk around with nothing but diapers!"

The serviceberry blew down in the blizzard of '78, ten years after the neighbor died. New shoots are now growing from the stump. The spring after the blizzard, a shellbark hickory sprouted several feet from the serviceberry, at the edge of the gateway between our farms, and today is at least thirty feet high. It should bear hickory nuts this year.

The predominant tree along the fencerow, though, is the wild cherry, and, as food for wildlife, it is the most important. In late summer and early fall many different kinds of animals feed on its abundant fruit. This includes the red and gray foxes, raccoons, skunks, opossums, and even deer. Sometimes when hauling wood from stacked piles in late fall, we discover caches of wild cherry pits that deer mice and chipmunks have stored for the winter. Birds, likewise, relish the cherries and feed heavily on them for a month or so. We use them ourselves to make a delicious jelly.

From April through July the fencerow rings with bird song. While we were plowing alongside it this spring, several song sparrows, a pair of bluebirds, and a cardinal entertained us. The bluebird nested in a box across the gateway from the hickory. Later, in May, I spotted a Tennessee warbler and other migrants.

Tonight, when we walked back to check our rain-starved crops, the fencerow belonged to the indigo bunting and the common yellowthroat. Both nest in the tangles of briars, and both sang all evening.

Bobwhites also nest in the grasses along the fencerow. A few weeks ago while cultivating corn, I heard a bobwhite calling almost constantly. But now that the female is incubating the eggs, the male is silent. Last winter a covey of quail made the fencerow their home territory. They fed on ragweed and other weed seeds and at night were sheltered from the marauding great horned owl and fox by the thick cover of the brambles. It was May before the covey split up and left in pairs to search for nesting places.

The most important mammal in the fencerow must be the woodchuck. By their penchant for digging burrows, the woodchucks do not provide homes only for themselves; when abandoned, the holes are used by many other mammals. Most skunks and many opossums, raccoons, and gray foxes live permanently in woodchuck burrows. Red foxes will also use the woodchuck's home to raise their pups. Should a woodchuck be in the burrow in late winter when the vixen decides on a location, the hapless animal is often killed when the fox takes over the den. Once a burrow becomes flea-infested, the young foxes are moved to a new den, where, very likely, another woodchuck will be kicked out.

Cottontails, too, and even pheasants and bobwhites will, in severe weather, seek the safety of a woodchuck hole.

Woodchucks do, however, eat hay crops, soybeans, garden vegetables, and sometimes young corn plants, and so they are despised by many farmers and gardeners. Thousands are shot each year by varmint hunters. But in spite of persecution by dogs, foxes, and hunters, this hearty animal is thriving. As long as there are fencerows, there will be woodchucks.

Fencerows often serve as travel lines for animals, especially deer and foxes, and on hillsides fencerows help to control erosion. Many fields on the uphill side of a fencerow are a foot or more higher than the field on the downhill side. Another benefit of the fencerow is that it is a renewable source of heat for the winter months. In a year or so the bigger trees in our fencerow can be cut and sawed into stove-lengths. For a fast-growing tree, seasoned cherry is a surprisingly good firewood. The wild cherry stumps will quickly sprout shoots, growing sometimes six to eight feet in the first year, and the cycle will be repeated. Cutting some of the trees will not greatly harm the value of the fencerow for wildlife, particularly if the brush is left in piles for additional cover.

Sadly, fencerows have become unfashionable. They began disappearing when the bulldozer became affordable, farm size increased, and the 2-4-D brush killers were developed. Soon after the demise of the fencerow, hunters began complaining about the scarcity of rabbits and pheasants. The blame was mistakenly put on the fox and the owl.

Last year the tenant farmer and I were talking across the fence when he suggested tearing out the fencerow. Since he enjoys the outdoors and deer hunting, I first mentioned the buck rubs, then the fox den, and the covey of quail, the serviceberry . . . We soon agreed that bulldozing this ribbon of life wasn't "cost effective."

The Rails

The bird appeared to be about the size of a meadowlark when it flushed in front of the mowing machine. It looked weak in flight, as it fluttered only a short distance, long legs dangling, suddenly to flop into the unmowed part of the third-crop hay. A round or two later it again flew and this time landed on the mowed hay. What seemed like weakness in flight was made up for by speed on the ground. In a flash, the bird raced back to the safety of the standing hay. I did, however, manage to get a good glimpse. A stubby tail, black-and-white barring on its flanks, rusty brown back, and a long slender, slightly down-curved bill convinced me that the bird was a Virginia rail.

This is only the third sighting of a Virginia rail on our farm, and all three birds were in hayfields. The first one, maybe ten years ago, looked almost as black as a starling as it flew away from the team and mower. I first thought it was a black rail, as I gawked at the departing bird. Then it dawned on me that this bird was much too large to be the sparrow-sized black rail of the salt marshes along the eastern seaboard. After consulting the field guide, I realized that it must have been an immature Virginia rail. The second one, several years later, gave us a much better look as it flew from the hay we were mowing and alighted in the pasture field. For as shy as rails are, this one allowed us within ten feet of where it was "hiding" in some short grass before it got nervous and took wing.

Rails may not be as uncommon as we think. Their secretive ways in the tall marsh vegetation and their reluctance to fly prevent us from seeing them very often. (Incidentally, it is legal to hunt rails during the fall months. The daily bag limit is twenty-five!)

We farmers often hear the term that an unthrifty animal is as "skinny as a rail." I always thought this saying referred to a split rail in a fence—that is, until I held a Virginia rail in my hand. A friend was trapping for muskrats one November and accidentally caught a Virginia rail in a conibear trap set in a 'rat run through cattails. When he showed me the bird, I was astounded at how small it looked in my hand compared to the flying ones in our hayfields. Another surprise was how "skinny" the rail was. Even with the wings folded to its sides the rail was hardly more than an inch wide across its chest, remarkably well suited, I thought, for a life of slipping between cattails and skulking in sedges.

The following summer we saw the first and only sora that we have seen on the farm. And, I grant, ours was not the most desirable of views—another bird-in-hand deal. This one was "collected" by a car in front of our house. I was taking a letter to the mailbox when I found the broken body, still warm, on the road. In typical rail fashion, the sora chose to run across the road rather than fly, and so got bashed. Again I was surprised at its small size, about like a horned lark or bobolink. It had a bright yellow chickenlike bill, yellowish green legs, black on the face and throat, and barring along the flanks of its grayish brown body. A very pretty bird indeed. Since the sora was an adult and it was June, I had to wonder if it had a mate and if they were nesting in the hayfield across from the mailbox. We found no signs of a nest or young. Or another sora. Since then, we have seen soras a number of times in marshes away from home.

The sora is the most common of the North American rails, followed in abundance by the Virginia. The largest of the rails is the king. It looks much like the Virginia but is twice as large.

Prior to 1930 the king rail was common along the larger bodies of water here in Ohio. Now it is a rare migrant and summer resident. We have never seen one. My brother and nephew once watched one of these chicken-sized rails as it searched for snails, frogs, and other aquatic life along the edge of a marsh bordering the Killbuck River.

Along the East and West Coasts the clapper rail is the saltwater version of the inland freshwater king rail. John James Audubon named these two rails the Salt-water Marsh Hen and the Fresh-water Marsh Hen. Similar to the king rail, the clapper is more washed-out in color. Where the two species overlap in Delaware and Virginia hybrids sometimes occur.

The brackish marshland of the East Coast, from New Jersey south, is home also to the black rail. This mouselike bird is extremely difficult to see and ranks high on many birders' "most wanted" list. No nests of the black rail were found from 1953 to 1985, when one was discovered on Elliot Island in Maryland. The nest had eight eggs, all of which hatched. Black rails are active at night, and bird-watchers have found that a tape recording of their call, played at night near a singing male, will sometimes bring him within range of a flashlight.

Farther inland, in the northern United States and Canada, the same means are used to lure the almost equally elusive yellow rail out from the wet sedge meadows it inhabits. Instead of a tape recording, two small stones are tapped together to imitate the clicking call of this small rail. The male, only a shade larger than the black rail, will often leave the thick cover to fight the supposed intruder and protect his nesting territory.

All rails lay large clutches of eggs, usually between seven and twelve. The sora has been known to lay eighteen. Following an incubation period of about twenty days, the young hatch and, being precocial, soon leave the nest with their mother. An ornithologist described the glossy black chicks of the Virginia rail: "Each looked like a tiny meatball banded with fluff, impossibly skewered on a pair of toothpicks that rapidly vibrated as the chick fluttered after its mother."

Although rails are reluctant to fly, they migrate surprisingly long distances to the southern United States and Central America. The sora has the longest migration route of the family, around three thousand miles each way. Once airborne, their mind set to their journey, the rails are strong fliers in migration. Every fall many congregate in the tidal marshes of the East Coast, where hunters will then stalk the Virginia rail and sora. The other species are protected. In years past, thousands were shot during high tides, which flooded the rails out of the cover of the tall marsh grasses.

I hope enough survive to stop over sometimes for rest and food in our hayfields, where we then might see these shy birds of the marshlands.

The Upland Sandpiper

During my boyhood years I would occasionally hear two mysterious birdcalls, usually coming from high in the sky on late spring and early summer evenings. One was songlike—a sweet, rich, musical trill, wild and hauntingly beautiful. The other was more of a call, a drawn-out whistle, first rising and then falling in pitch. At times it sounded more like the whistling of the wind than a bird's voice.

Some years passed before I realized that the song and whistle came from the same bird. And some more time went by before I came to know that the maker of the music was an upland sandpiper. This happened almost by chance. I flushed an upland sandpiper, and as it alighted on a fencepost, the graceful bird held its wings outstretched high over its back for a moment or two before carefully folding them. Then it whistled the call I had heard for years. I wasn't disappointed. A bird as serene and graceful and rare as the upland sandpiper should have a wild and mysterious song.

Back in those days this inland shorebird was called the upland plover. Though truly a sandpiper, its habits of nesting in hayfields, meadows, and prairies away from water are more like those of a plover. (The killdeer is a plover.) I regretted the name change. The new name may be more accurate, but to me it just doesn't seem right. Maybe it lacks the mystery I associate with the bird.

The upland sandpiper is a bit larger than the killdeer. It is fairly easily recognizable by its color, size, and shape: brown, streaked plumage, small dovelike head, long neck, and short yellow bill. It also has a long tail for a shorebird. Probably the best identification point is its unique habit of holding its wings elevated upon landing. This brief pose is particularly pretty. As Aldo Leopold wrote, "Whoever invented the word 'grace' must have seen the wing folding of the plover."

Arriving on their nesting grounds at this latitude in early to mid-April, the female will, by the end of the month, lay four eggs, cream to pink-buff speckled with brown or red, in a grass-lined nest. The nest is often made in a slight hollow in the ground and well hidden by long, thick grass.

Following an incubation period of twenty-one to twenty-four days, the young hatch and, being precocial, soon leave the nest attended by the parents. Growing rapidly on a diet of grasshoppers, crickets, and weevils, the young are fully grown and flying in a month. On July evenings their calls can be heard as they prepare to migrate to the pampas of Argentina.

These gentle birds almost suffered the same fate as the passenger pigeons. In the late 1800s, as the pigeons were exterminated, the guns were turned toward shorebirds. Hunters on horseback and in wagons, armed with shotguns, roamed the prairies and shipped hundreds of barrels of plovers, curlews, and sandpipers to eastern markets.

In 1919 Dr. Thomas S. Roberts of Minnesota wrote about the plight of the upland sandpiper: "Fifty years ago it was present all through summer, everywhere in open country, in countless thousands. Now it is nearing extinction. Here and there an occasional breeding pair may yet be found, but they are lonely occupants of the places where their ancestors dwelt in vast numbers."

The signing of the Migratory Bird Treaty Act by President Woodrow Wilson in 1918 came in the nick of time for many shorebirds. This treaty gave the United States and Canadian governments the power to establish a closed season, prohibiting the killing of threatened species such as the upland sandpiper. With full protection their numbers built up, but never to their precarnage populations. Maybe changes in farming practices are partly to blame for the birds' current scarcity, especially the practice of cutting hay while the birds are still nesting. Interestingly, the strongest colony of these sandpipers extant in New York State is at Kennedy Airport, surely a man-altered environment.

Last year we saw only one of these charming birds. The two youngest children and I were on our way to Mt. Hope to get binder twine when we spotted an upland sandpiper perched on the telephone cable just north of town. Finishing our business, we hurried back. The bird was still there, and so we stopped for a better look. It seemed unafraid as it perched ten feet above us. My guess is that it was a newly flying young bird because the older birds are much more wary.

Bruce Stambaugh, principal at the Mt. Hope school, told me that he saw a pair of sandpipers south of the schoolhouse the year before, near where we saw the one sitting on the cable. All of this small farm is in pasture and is not mowed until mid-summer. A perfect nesting place for these birds.

The upland sandpipers probably were never as abundant here in the East as they were or are in the prairie lands of the central United States and Canada. But what we had we treasured, and it is with sadness that we watch their numbers gradually dwindle here. Just this spring a friend from Wayne County lamented the disappearance of the sandpipers from his neighborhood. He misses the thrill of glimpsing those uplifted wings.

Life in
the Marsh

John James Audubon, who long dreamed of visiting the Everglades, had second thoughts when he got his first look at the swamp-bound St. Johns River. He wrote in his journal, "Here I am in the Floridas . . . which from my childhood I have consecrated in my imagination as a garden of the United States. A garden where all that is not mud, mud, mud, is sand, sand, sand; where the fruit is so sour that it is not eatable, and in place of singing birds and golden fishes, you have . . . alligators, snakes, and scorpions."

On the other hand, George Washington was fascinated by Virginia's Great Dismal Swamp and described it as a "glorious paradise."

I'd have to agree with the latter view, though the swamps and marshes I'm acquainted with are a far cry from the Everglades or the Great Dismal. Nevertheless, to me, born and raised an "uplander," the wetlands along the Killbuck River have always had an exciting appeal. During my boyhood I'd listen with rapt attention to stories about this mysterious place—of teal flying so swiftly they couldn't be shot, snapping turtles the size of bushel baskets, long-legged swamp coons that wouldn't hesitate to jump into the icy river and swim half a mile downstream to evade the hounds, carp as long as a neck yoke. Here were wild things that were foreign to me, and I couldn't wait to see them for myself. We were fortunate to have friends, the Weavers and Masts, who owned land next to the Killbuck and gladly gave us permission to explore the hinterlands of their farms.

The Killbuck River, named after Chief Killbuck of the Delaware Indians, and the narrow valley through which it flows are rich in history. Indian towns and villages were scattered all along the river throughout the 1700s. One of these, Killbuck's Town, was within what is now the forty-five-hundred-acre Killbuck Marsh Wildlife Area. It was located about a mile south of County Line Road near the fording place of the Killbuck. This fording place remains to this day, and when the river is low, we can easily wade across it.

Killbuck's Town was home to Chief Killbuck for a while, and at one time the treaty papers signed by William Penn with the Delawares were kept here. Across the marsh from the town was Butler's, or the Big Spring. Here Colonel William Crawford and his army of 480 men camped on the night of May 30, 1782. The next morning they forded the Killbuck en route to their ill-fated encounter with the Wyandot Indians.

Gradually, with the coming of the Europeans, the Indians were forced from their beloved Killbuck Valley. Up until 1900 the river and marshes had changed very little. Then, around 1923 or '24, a steam shovel on a barge, beginning in the vicinity of Wooster, steadily ate its way downriver until it reached the village of present-day Killbuck. All the oxbows were straightened and the meandering river was no more. The water now flowed straight as an arrow. One of the purposes of this endeavor was to drain the wetlands so that they could be farmed.

Many of these drainage attempts ended in failure. Today one can still see the tops of fenceposts in parts of the marsh. The river has again reclaimed these fields for its own, fields that probably never should have been. The old B&O railroad bed that runs parallel to the river through the swamps is also slowly giving way to the forces of nature.

The marshes along the Killbuck seem barren and lifeless during the winter months, but they suddenly burst with life in the spring, as thousands of ducks pass through on migration in March and early April.

The most common resident duck is the wood duck which, in my opinion, is the most beautiful waterfowl in North America. This cavity-nesting duck can be seen regularly until ice covers the marshes in early winter. (Some parts of the marshes that are fed by strong springs never freeze, and a few hardy ducks may stay all winter on these open spots of water.) The past several years, some hooded mergansers also have stayed and raised young in the area. These flashy birds also nest in wood duck boxes. And of course mallards, possibly some blue-winged teal, and Canada geese also nest there.

The ducks are only a small part of the birdlife in the marshes. A few miles south of the abundant wildlife area in a grove of sycamore trees is a rookery of great blue herons. Green-backed herons, American bitterns, sora and Virginia rails, common moorhens, and American coots can also be seen occasionally.

As spring advances the wild cry of the red-shouldered hawk, "kill-yer, kill-yer, kill-yer," can be heard in the wooded parts of the swamps. The barred owl too is at home in the flooded river bottom. At night its "who-cooks-for-you-all" carries across the marshes. Likewise, the little screech owl is a frequent nester in houses meant for wood ducks.

One warbler which we have never seen on our farm, but which is common in the lowlands, is the prothonotary. This brilliant golden yellow warbler seldom nests far from water. Sometimes their nesting cavity is only inches above the water and rarely higher than fifteen feet.

Several years ago a friend was standing on a beaver dam when a male prothonotary warbler alighted about twenty feet in front of him on a tree limb that extended into the water. The bird inched down the branch and was just ready to take a drink when there was a mighty splash as a northern pike lunged at it. The warbler escaped.

Another small bird that nests over water in the wetlands is the ruby-throated hummingbird. Once, while floating down the river in a canoe when the water was several feet above normal, we found two hummingbird nests at eye level, almost on the very tips of silver maple twigs.

The swamp sparrow is at home in the wetlands' cattails and reeds, whereas the song sparrow sticks to the edges. Likewise, the Carolina wren's rollicking song can be heard in the thickets surrounding the marshes, while its kin the marsh wren nests in the cattails. I'll not soon forget my first sight of a marsh wren. I discovered not only the elusive bird but also the old channel of the Killbuck. We saw a small bird in a clump of button-bushes some distance in the marsh. Since I was wearing hip boots, I volunteered to wade through the spatterdock to check out the bird. All went well until I reached a place where there was no spatterdock. I could see mud a foot beneath the water's surface, so I thought it seemed safe enough. I plunged in and promptly sank several inches deeper than my boots were high. My feet were wet anyhow so I went on through and was pleased to see not one but two marsh wrens. (I soon learned to tread gingerly where there was no vegetation. In some of these ox-bows of the old river channel you can push a canoe paddle down as far as you can reach and still not touch bottom.)

With the coming of summer and the completion of the nesting season for most birds, the marsh now seems to belong to the frogs, reptiles, and mosquitoes. Besides the common nonpoisonous northern water snake, the poisonous massasauga, or swamp rattlesnake, has been seen in the wildlife area. John Staab told me that in his years as wildlife manager for the area he saw only two of the small rattlers. The first one was in the driveway of his home and the other one on the old railroad bed.

When summer fades into autumn, the mammals of the marshes become more noticeable as they prepare for winter. Once frost has killed most of the marsh plants, muskrat houses begin to show as brown humps throughout the marshes. The beavers, too, are busy gathering food for winter. These ingenious workers do a remarkable job of restoring many acres of marginal land to marsh again. Their work would help make Chief Killbuck feel at home were he to come paddling silently again down the river that bears his name.

Autumn is also the time for the white-tailed deer to become active as the rutting season approaches. With its rusty summer coat now changed to match the grays and browns of the marsh grasses, the crafty animal is a match for any hunter who dares venture into the mud and tangles of the swamps.

When at last ice covers the marshes in late December, they again appear lifeless. However, this is far from true. The muskrats and beavers still leave their houses and lodges and swim underwater to "feedbeds" for nourishment. The mink is on the prowl for muskrat. The frogs and turtles are alive and well, burrowed deep in the mud, awaiting spring.

My memories of marshes are pleasant—a flash of yellow as a prothonotary darts across the river on a May morning, canoeing on a warm summer night looking for frogs, sharing a hot drink with a friend in the crispness of late fall. Washington was right, a swamp is a "glorious paradise."

When I think of marshes I'm reminded of Sidney Lanier's beautiful poem *The Marshes of Glynn*, which goes in part:

> And now from the Vast of the Lord will the waters of sleep
> Roll in on the souls of men,
> But who will reveal to our waking ken
> The forms that swim and the shapes that creep
> Under the waters of sleep?

The Wings
of Summer Nights

Last summer the children discovered the larva of a cecropia moth on the Cortland apple tree in our garden patch. The tree was young, only in its third summer, so the caterpillar was fairly easy to find and observe. Even then, if it remained motionless, it was sometimes difficult to locate among the green leaves. We checked daily on the hungry worm as it continued to eat and grow and grow and grow!

As the time approached for the caterpillar to pupate, it began showing a growing restlessness. The worm was now close to five inches long. As it slowly crawled along the slender twigs of the apple tree, one of the children remarked, "It's almost as big as a hot dog. Yuck! A green one." Our hopes of seeing the larva spin its silken cocoon were dashed when it left the tree during the next night. Later on in the fall, when the apple trees lost their leaves, I found the papery, puffy, double-walled cocoon attached along one entire side to a branch of the McIntosh apple tree, a good hundred feet from where it had eaten its last meal on the Cortland.

The cecropia, sometimes called Robin moth, is the biggest member of the silk moth family. After it emerges from the cocoon in late spring or early summer, its wings look crumpled and wilted. But as the moth pumps fluid into them, the wings begin to expand and dry. Once fully expanded, the cecropia may have a wingspan of six inches. With its red-orange body and gray-brownish wings highlighted by rusty orange and white crescents and a tawny outer margin, this moth is one of the most richly textured and beautiful insects in the world.

Several years ago we watched as a cecropia caterpillar spun and attached its cocoon to the siding of our porch. The following summer we happened to see the moth emerge from the cocoon. After its wings had hardened, we gently moved it to the maple tree where, accented by the dark bark, its colors and beauty cannot be fittingly described. To our good fortune the moth was a female. We could tell by her feathery feelers, which were narrower than the wide plumelike antennae of the males. It is with these antennae that cecropias locate mates. Edwin Way Teale writes, "The great fernlike feelers of the Cecropia and Polyphemus moths provide these night-flying insects with smelling organs infinitely more sensitive than the nose of the most keen-scented bloodhound. After moths have been marked and released, they have proved their ability to follow faint scent trails through the air for seven miles and more in order to reach the location of a virgin female."

Our female moth was content to remain on the maple tree as if she was expecting company. I got up during the night and with a flashlight discovered that the suitors had arrived. A dozen or more of the batlike moths fluttered about the tree momentarily blinded by the light. By morning only one male remained. The others had followed scent trails elsewhere.

A day or two later the female began laying her two hundred to three hundred jewel-like eggs, which started hatching shortly thereafter. About a week after emerging from her cocoon, the female died. During the short span of their adult lives, the moths do not eat. Their last meal was eaten ten months ago!

Besides the cecropia, there are other equally beautiful silk moths fluttering around on summer nights: the polyphemus, promethea, luna, and Io. The imported Cynthia moth is fairly common along the Atlantic coast. Since it feeds solely on the leaves of ailanthus trees, also known as tree-of-heaven, this moth is confined to the cities where these trees grow profusely in vacant lots, parks, and along railroad tracks.

The polyphemus and promethea are common here on our farm. We have a Chinese elm in our yard, and at the base of this tree we often find the polyphemus cocoons. In its larval stage this strikingly colored moth feeds on elm, apple, maple, oak, and other shade trees. One year, almost as if on cue, several dozen polyphemus caterpillars came crawling across the lawn, across the siding of the house, and along the walks to an ever-green shrub beside our porch steps. This occurred over a pe-riod of two days. There within the shrub and on the leaf litter beneath it they spun themselves into cocoons. The caterpillars began with a single strand of silk and rolled their heads around and around until they disappeared from sight, woven within a cocoon that contained from one to five miles of silken thread. This shrub proved to be a good location, safe from woodpeck-ers and other enemies. Needless to say, the next year we had a lot of polyphemus moths to enjoy.

In a way I wished this phenomenon had happened while I was still in school, when we had annual contests to see which pupil could find the most cocoons of the three common spe-cies. Our teacher, C. F. Zuercher, had a point system worked out: each promethea cocoon, considered the most common, counted five points, the cecropia twenty-five points, and the polyphemus fifty. Anyone finding twenty or more fifty-pointers would have been a sure winner. (The reason the po-lyphemus cocoons are hard to find is that they're often on the ground and blend in well with the leaves.)

The delicate pale green luna moth with its swallow-tailed wings, likewise, in its larval stage spins its cocoon and drops to the ground where it lies buried in the debris beneath oak, hick-ory, sweetgum, and persimmon trees, to emerge the following year. The luna has been called our most beautiful insect, and because of its scarcity it is now considered an endangered species. For years I have longed to see a luna moth up close. Once we found one dead in a neighbor's woods, and so I know there are a few around. And twice I have seen live ones, but neither gave me the opportunity for close-up viewing and appreciation. We were riding in an automobile when we saw our first luna moth. My wife spotted one on the screened door of a house as the moth was attempting to reach the light inside. The other one I saw fluttering around a mercury-vapor light in town. Although I was tempted, I refrained from climbing the pole for a better look.

Finally, in my desperation, I sent away for five luna cocoons from a butterfly farm that had advertised in an outdoor magazine. When they arrived in the mail, only one of the five showed signs of life. I could hear a faint stirring when I gently shook the cocoon. My hopes soared. However, I was in for more disappointment. Upon emerging from the cocoon, its wings never filled and spread. Instead, they hardened in their wrinkled position, making the poor moth look like a lime green prune.

The promethea, or spicebush moth, is as common as the luna is rare. They feed on spicebush, sassafras, and wild cherry, the trees where their cocoons are generally found. The caterpillars spin their cocoons within a leaf. They begin by spinning silk around the twig to which the leaf is attached, then work their way down the leaf stem until they reach the leaf. The caterpillar then encloses itself, and remains suspended there through the winter months. When we were in school, we knew every good sassafras and wild cherry fencerow around, because there we could be sure to find a bunch of five-pointers.

The promethea moths differ from others in the silk moth family in that the males and females are of different colors. The males are brownish black with faint spots while the females are similarly marked but are reddish brown, more like the cecropia, and are thus more colorful. Moreover, the males begin flying in late afternoon and are frequently eaten by purple martins and other birds. The females fly only at night.

I suspect that quite a few farmers are familiar with the caterpillar of the Io moth. In its larval stage the Io often feeds in cornfields, and many of us farmers have at one time or another had a "cornworm" down the inside of our shirt. The spines on this caterpillar cause a painful stinging similar to nettle, only much worse. Outside of an occasional encounter with a "cornworm," the larvae of the pretty silk moths are seldom harmful.

In many parts of the country the silk moths are disappearing. No one is sure of the reasons why, but they likely include destruction of habitat, the overuse of pesticides, and, as some experts insist, the effects of sodium and mercury lights around homes and along streets and highways. The large imperial moth, for instance, has a weakness for artificial light. It is attracted to the lights and often lingers into daylight when it is then eaten by birds. This moth is becoming rare where artificial lights are abundant.

It is amazing that the huge green cecropia larva on our apple tree, with its many segments and legs, could spin itself inside a cocoon, and while doing so already begin to shrink in size— to reappear ten months later, without having eaten a bite, a fully developed insect with three segments and three pairs of legs, one of the most beautiful creatures in God's Creation. I can't comprehend a change so complex and so complete. When I think of it I feel like Ezra: "And when I heard this thing, I rent my garment and my mantle, and plucked off the hair of my head and my beard and sat down astonied."

The World
of Insects

With the coming of August most of our birds have ceased their singing. During the early summer about the only night sounds are the trilling calls of the gray tree frogs and the occasional hoot of a great horned owl. Now the singing insects take center stage. During the daylight hours the cicadas and grasshoppers entertain us with their raspy, buzzing music, while at night there is a mixed chorus of katydids and various crickets.

Insects are lovers of heat. The warmer the days and nights, the more vehement their music becomes.

Many of the hundreds of thousands of insects in our world are helpful or at least not harmful to mankind. Actually, without insects, life as we know it may not be possible. They are important pollinators of fruits and vegetables, they help in fertilizing the soil, and they provide such commercially valuable products as honey, beeswax, and silk. Although insects are the most numerous creatures on earth (excluding microscopic life), there is much we don't know about them. Edwin Way Teale wrote, "An insect breathes but has no lungs. It hears but has no ears on its head. It smells but has no nose. Its heart pumps blood but it is so unlike our hearts that it often reverses itself and beats backward. From birth to death, it is a creature of strange habits and puzzling abilities, a creature surrounded by mystery."

Even insects we regard as common are still startling when

we see them up close. The praying mantis, for example, familiar to us as an asset in the garden, is indeed strange to behold. Its way of gazing over its shoulder to watch us is uncanny; it is the only insect that can turn its head like a man. Last summer we watched a mantis feast on a wooly bear caterpillar, and after it had crunched up the last shred of its victim, it cleaned its smooth green face like a cat.

Adult mantises eat more or less everything that comes within reach. Their main diet consists of beetles, bugs, caterpillars, and other insects. While it is fearless and combative, it is entirely harmless to humans.

In late spring when the days grow warmer and longer, the young mantises hatch from foamy egg cases. Each egg case can contain from 125 to 350 young mantises. The newly hatched insects are soft, defenseless, and honey yellow in color. About fifteen minutes later their skin has hardened, and the color has changed to light brown. They are now ready to begin their lives as hunters. During the first days of their lives, they eat small creatures, such as plant lice, and will not hesitate to dine on each other. In fact, if they hatch in confined quarters such as a mason jar, they will devour each other until only one remains.

Throughout the summer each mantis is a loner. It searches for its own food and exists by its own skill. In this region, these insects go through their final molt in August. Following this molt, their slender, gauzy wings appear. They are now fully grown. The time of year is now approaching when mating takes place, followed by a strange feast. The female eats her mate! The French entomologist J. Henri Fabre, who devoted his life to the study of insects, says that a female mantis may mate with and consume up to seven males. Following her bizarre feast, she produces the froth case which contains the eggs.

One autumn when I was still in school, some of us students found an obviously about-to-lay female mantis. The corpulent creature was taken to the schoolroom and released on a bouquet of goldenrod. Shortly afterward, hanging head-down, she began moving her tail back and forth, producing a white, foamy mass in an expanding circle much in the same way that a threshing machine makes a straw stack. When the egg case was almost completed, she paused and laid her eggs within it and then added some more foam to finish up. The entire process took the better part of two hours.

The praying mantis is noticeable because of its size, but some of the other insects, such as the katydid, are heard more often than seen. The katydid is a handsome insect which resembles a grasshopper but is a brilliant green, with a slightly humped back and long, graceful antennae. All katydids are night singers, and their music (a loud two-part "katy-DID" or the less often heard three-part "katy-DIDN'T") is made by lifting the wings and running the edge of one over the other. One wing cover is equipped with a scraper, the other with a file, and the sound is produced in much the same fashion as scraping a knife across a file.

In the base of their wings katydids possess a miniature amplifier that gives enormous projection. Less than one-eighth-inch across, this disc-shaped device is made of chitin, or the stuff from which the strong outside skeleton of the insect is made. It is thinner than paper but stronger than a comparable thickness of steel. And what is most astonishing is that this tiny megaphone can amplify an almost inaudible scratch into a loud "katy-DID" that can carry, on a calm quiet night, for nearly half a mile.

Closely related to the katydid are the many species of crickets. One of these, the snowy tree cricket, not only entertains us with its musical chirps, but, surprisingly, can tell us the temperature. The tree crickets sing in unison and are so well synchronized that as you travel down a country road it seems as if you're hearing only one of the delicate green insects singing.

Henry Thoreau called it a "slumberous breathing." The warmer the weather, the more rapid the chirps. Their notes are so consistent that a formula has been worked out by which one can fairly accurately tell the temperature. Count the number of chirps in fifteen seconds and add forty. The total is the temperature in degrees Fahrenheit.

Insects that we notice because of their beauty are the butterflies. One that is frequently seen around our farm is the monarch. These beautiful black-veined orange butterflies, unlike the many other butterfly species, fly south in the fall much like many of our birds. It has been known for a century that monarchs overwinter in California, but it wasn't until 1975 that the wintering grounds of the monarchs of the eastern two-thirds of our continent were discovered in the Sierra Chinqua Mountains in Mexico. After he spent forty years developing a tagging program, Professor Fred Urquhart of the University of Toronto found the Mexican wintering grounds. We marvel at the vast distances the golden plovers and Arctic terns migrate, but that a fragile butterfly should travel several thousand miles seems almost miraculous.

After spending the winter in the Mexican mountains, their journey north begins about the time of the spring equinox. Many will die on the return trip, but not before laying eggs along the way. And it is their offspring that arrive on our farm sometime in late spring.

The monarch always lays its eggs on milkweeds, usually on the underside of the leaves near the midrib, and they resemble green-tinted drops of dew. After four or five days the egg opens, and a tiny caterpillar appears and begins feeding on the milkweed leaves. In about a dozen days the brilliantly marked, yellow, black, and green caterpillar has reached its full size of about two inches in length. It is now time to pupate. The caterpillar may crawl several hundred feet from the plant on which it last fed. Finding a suitable twig or plant—we frequently find their chrysalises on stalks of oats while shocking or threshing—and then spinning silk from glands in its mouth, it attaches its tail to the underside. Hanging downward, curving its head upward to form a letter J, the larva slowly changes form. The pupa, or chrysalis, hardens and remains hanging by a thread of silk. Unlike the drab-looking chrysalises of most butterflies, the monarch's is a work of art. Smooth and waxy green, it is decorated with spots of shining gold.

After twelve days the chrysalis opens on the bottom, and an adult monarch butterfly emerges. It clings to a twig or leaf until its wings expand and harden. If it is late summer, it will soon begin the long journey to Mexico, feeding on the nectar of flowers along the way.

Strangely enough, birds never eat monarchs. Beneath our martin houses we find different species of butterflies that were brought to feed the young, but never monarchs. It is thought that they have bad-tasting blood which nauseates the birds that try to eat them.

Because of the birds' aversion to the monarch, another butterfly from a different family, the viceroy, is also immune to their attacks. It so closely resembles the monarch that birds avoid it. Though less common than the monarch, we usually see several viceroys when mowing our pasture fields, as they flit from flower to flower of the tall joe-pye weeds.

The list of fascinating insects is almost endless. Consider ants, for example. Even Solomon wrote about the ant, "consider her ways, and be wise." Certain colonies of ants keep tiny aphids, the way we keep cows, feed them choice food, and harvest the honeydew that the aphids produce. Robber ants are known to go on raids and steal the pupae of other ant species and carry them home. When these pupae hatch, they serve their kidnappers as slaves. This has been going on for so long that the robber ants have forgotten how to work.

Or consider the click beetle which, when flicked onto its back, will cock its head and snap it so hard that it will fly as much as a foot into the air. Should the beetle land on its back again, the process is repeated until it alights on its feet.

The May fly is another intriguing creature. It may emerge as an adult in the evening, mate, lay its eggs, and die before sunrise, all this accomplished without ever eating.

In studying insects, a good field guide is indispensable, such as *Peterson's Field Guide to Insects* or *The Audubon Society Field Guide to North American Insects and Spiders*, which we prefer.

Maybe we should take more time to study this fascinating part of God's Creation instead of swatting and spraying everything that crosses our path. It's hard, I admit, to appreciate potato bugs and green-headed horse flies, but few sounds can compare with an orchestra of katydids and myriads of crickets on a warm August night.

Butterflies

With the wheat and oats harvest over, the pace of summer slows down. Urgency has been replaced by a sweet serenity, a lingering before the season of corn harvest. A friend claims that when the winds blow over the oats stubble, though we're still in the dog days, he can already feel the pulse of autumn, a season he so dearly loves that, when it does arrive, he's moved to write poetry.

The last blackberries are ripening, and as we pick them, the loud unmusical song of the yellow-breasted chat that had entertained us while picking raspberries in June has been replaced by the raspy calls of cicadas, its beauty by that of butterflies.

Along with the blackberries in my favorite field-returning-to-forest are numerous wildflowers. The first goldenrods are just coming into bloom, while the iron and joe-pye weeds, dogbane, Queen Anne's lace, milkweeds, and a late-blooming butterfly weed have all been adding color and offering nectar to a parade of butterflies for most of the summer.

The butterfly weed, a member of the milkweed family, is a favorite of the monarch and fritillary butterflies. I have seen up to five fritillaries, usually the great spangled, but occasionally a regal or variegated, feeding on the bright orange clusters of flowers at one time. Of course, other species of butterflies are also attracted to this plant.

Its near relative, the swamp milkweed, is almost as attractive to butterflies. As the name implies, it grows in wetlands and along streams. Monarchs and viceroys frequent the clusters of dusty rose blossoms. For some reason, maybe because of its proximity to water, or because they are searching for aphids, which live and feed on the plant, damsel flies also often rest on this lovely milkweed.

Among the most striking butterflies, as they flutter among the majestic purple blooms of the ironweeds, are the swallowtails. The most common of this extended family is the tiger swallowtail. This large yellow butterfly with black tigerlike stripes occurs throughout the eastern United States. Some of the females of this species are dark colored, especially in the southern part of its range.

The eastern black swallowtail looks similar to the dark-phase female tiger swallowtail, but the habits of their larvae are very different. Whereas the caterpillars of the tiger feed on wild cherry, ash, and poplar trees, the blacks feed on the foliage of the carrot family. This includes not only Queen Anne's lace (wild carrot) but also garden carrots, celery, and parsley. Hence the butterfly's other name, parsley swallowtail.

Two other swallowtails we occasionally see are the pipevine and spicebush. Though quite rare around here, these two are more common in the southern part of their range.

To me, the pipevine swallowtail is one of the most beautiful of all butterflies. Its black upper wings fade to an iridescent blue-green along the edges, while the hind wings fade to an even lighter blue-green. The back edges of the wings are then trimmed with tiny white crescents. Perhaps because of its rarity, this exquisite creature seems somehow exotic.

The spicebush swallowtail is more common in this area than is the pipevine, largely because it includes sassafras leaves in addition to spicebush as a favorite food in its larval stage. Pipevine larvae eat only Virginia snakeroot and Dutchman's pipe. The spicebush also has blue-green on its lower back wings but, unlike the pipevine, it has large yellow crescents along the borders of its wings.

I rarely see the giant or zebra swallowtails, which seldom venture this far north because of their preferences for certain foods not found here. The giant likes citrus orchards, and the zebra caterpillar eats only pawpaw leaves. I've known of only one pawpaw tree in our community, and that was lost when the woods were cut out.

Quite a few other butterflies are also what experts call "host-specific," meaning that while in their larval stage they will feed on just one kind of plant. The monarch, for instance, will lay its eggs only on milkweed, as will the queen butterfly in the South.

Unlike monarchs, most butterflies die in the fall. Their succeeding generation overwinters in the chrysalis, much as the silk moths do in their cocoons. Only a few species hibernate as adults, notably the red admiral and the mourning cloak.

Almost every winter there is a red admiral in our shop. On cold mornings it can be found on the windowsill or workbench, wings tightly folded and seemingly lifeless. But when the barrel stove is fired up, the little butterfly suddenly comes alive and flutters from window to window in its attempt to get outside. The mourning cloak is considered the first butterfly of the spring. It hibernates in hollow trees and logs and is sometimes seen flying on warm late winter days. For this reason the mourning cloak is sometimes called the "thaw butterfly." This somber-colored butterfly has become less common over the past three decades, possibly because of indiscriminate use of insecticides. The female lays her eggs on willow, elm, and poplar; her caterpillars can become pests since they feed in groups and can defoliate trees.

The day before yesterday I noticed that something was eating the leaves of our pussy willow. Upon checking, I found around three dozen mourning cloak caterpillars. The black red-dotted worms were feeding in three groups and had probably eaten about a fourth of the willow's leaves. Since I had often, over the years, bemoaned the decline of the mourning cloak, I was only too happy to let them eat the leaves. The caterpillars were big enough to enter the next stage of their metamorphosis in becoming butterflies. When I checked that evening, every larva was gone! Had I disturbed them and caused them to go elsewhere to feed? My guess is that the caterpillars' biological clock told them it was time to pupate.

Last evening we discovered one of the two-and-a-half-inch-long worms hanging from the bottom edge of our porch siding. It had crawled over a hundred feet from the pussy willow, across the lawn and lane, to reach the porch. The larva had already attached its tail to the siding and was hanging downward, its head turned up so its body formed a capital J. Sometime during the night the larva split its skin and worked it upward until the skin was off its body. The emerging pupa hardened in the night air and remained hanging from the tiny black thread fastened to the siding. This morning I immediately checked and found, instead of a black caterpillar, a perfectly formed one-inch-long gray mourning-cloak chrysalis. I never fail to be astounded by this incredible event.

If the larvae of the mourning cloak and black swallowtail do some damage, it is minor in comparison to an alien butterfly, the European cabbage butterfly. This little white insect was introduced accidentally in 1860 near Montreal, Quebec. From there it spread across North America. This is the only butterfly doing serious damage in our gardens, and I'm sure every gardener raising cabbage knows its slender green larvae. They attack not only cabbage but also many other related plants.

One morning last spring, coming in from the morning chores, I stopped by the garden and watched as a pair of chipping sparrows searched for cabbage worms. One sparrow started from my end of the row of cauliflower while its mate worked down from the far end. Each plant was diligently searched until the birds' bills were filled with the green pests. Then they flew to the nest and quickly returned satisfied that not a single worm had escaped them.

There is a biological control, *Bacillus thuringiensis* (BT), available for cabbage loopers. It is sold under the trade name of Dipel, a dust, and Thuricide, a liquid. We find the dust provides better control, because the liquid tends to ball and roll off the waxy cabbage leaves. BT is not a poison, and so it doesn't harm the chipping sparrows.

Similar to the cabbage butterfly are the orange and clouded sulfurs. At times dozens of these brightly colored butterflies congregate around a water puddle. Gardeners seldom consider them pests.

There are many other beautiful and interesting butterflies to be seen. In fact, there are over twelve thousand species of butterflies and moths in North America. Although many will feed on only a single species of plant in their larval stage, as adults they will feed on the nectar of a variety of flowers. In his excellent book *Wildlife in Your Garden*, Gene Logsdon lists a dozen plant groups that are especially attractive to butterflies. Our own experience has been that the butterfly weed is excellent, its only disadvantage being that it blooms for less than a month. Bee balm and wild bergamot, both in the mint family, are also preferred fare. This year we planted Mexican sunflowers, which are proving quite attractive, particularly to the fritillaries.

By far our best success has been the butterfly bush (*Buddleia davidii*). The fast-growing plant has spiked clusters of pinkish lavender flowers that begin to open in late July and bloom until frost. A wide range of butterflies visit the bush daily.

Butterflies may seem fragile, and in a sense they are, but to me few things are more wondrous than a crisp, newly hatched monarch feeding on a fresh spray of goldenrod on a late-summer morning; this, and the realization that the spectacular creature will then fly thousands of miles for the winter.

Fall

The Waterfowl Flyways

On the morning of a clear, cool autumn day, we brought the horses in early from the pasture. The rains had finally ended, and we hoped, at last, to finish sowing the wheat. While we were still in the pasture field, the first flocks of ducks came into the pond. Riding the currents of a brisk north wind, the ducks were flying high and incredibly fast. Then suddenly they side-slipped, like falling maple leaves, and dropped rapidly to the pond.

After taking the horses to the barn, I was on my way to the house for breakfast when I heard the distant calls of Canada geese. I didn't have long to wait until I saw the flock come winging in over the woods. Unlike ducks, these great birds seldom land downwind. They flew past the buildings and then circled, came in low, and landed in the cornfield across the road. Soon more geese arrived, and before long the field was ringing with their excited clamor. These geese are probably Ohio-raised and haven't yet traveled far in their southward journey. The ducks, however, have likely come quite a distance. I noticed this morning that there were some black ducks in the flocks as they whizzed overhead. Most of the black ducks nest from central Canada east to the maritime provinces and then fly south in the fall.

Every autumn when frost returns to the northern lakes and marshes, the waterfowl grow restless. From the prairies of the northern United States and Canada, north to Churchill on Hudson's Bay, to Baffin Island, west across the vast regions of the Northwest Territories, the Yukon, and Alaska, millions of ducks, geese, and swans are preparing to fly south for the winter.

These multitudes of waterfowl tend to travel along distinct routes. Wildlife biologists call these routes "flyways." There are four flyways: the Atlantic, Mississippi, Central, and Pacific. Although these migration flyways are fairly distinct at their southernmost points, they are vague and tend to overlap in the north. Thus the black ducks feeding in our field right now may have been hatched in Quebec and by December may be in the Gulf States, whereas a canvasback raised in the prairie pothole region of Manitoba will likely travel southeast across the Great Lakes to its chief wintering area along Chesapeake Bay.

By dividing the migration corridors into four flyways, the U.S. Fish and Wildlife Service can better determine the length of the hunting season each fall and set the bag limits for various species. For the past several seasons hunters waiting in the marshes have had fewer ducks to shoot at because the number of ducks is dwindling. The biologists, of course, can't agree on the reason for the decline, but they do agree on its seriousness.

As late as the fall of 1975, an estimated 100 million ducks, geese, and swans left their nesting grounds for the trip south. Last fall the estimates had dropped to 60 million. What particularly alarms the waterfowl managers is the decline of the species long considered to be stable, the mallards of the Mississippi and Central flyways and the pintail along the Pacific flyway. The pintail, called "sprig" by waterfowlers, is the bread-and-butter bird for California duck hunters. Nobody is more aware of this graceful duck's decline than they are. In 1980, 608,000 were shot by California gunners. In four years the annual kill had dropped to 191,000. Possible reasons for the decrease are the dry summers in the prairie pothole regions (considered the duck hatcheries of North America), drainage of wetlands, and overhunting. This last issue is cause for continuing disagreement between the Fish and Wildlife Service, which wants to shorten hunting seasons and reduce bag limits, and Ducks Unlimited, a private organization made up primarily of duck hunters devoted to habitat improvement. The latter claims that hunting has little significance on duck numbers. Could there be a possible connection between this decade's drastic decline of ducks and the fact that simultaneously the use of agricultural pesticides has more than doubled?

The canvasback, the largest and fastest of wild ducks, has fallen on hard times. Less than half a million of the regal birds exist in North America. For some unexplained reason, two out of three of those remaining are drakes. One possibility is that the raccoon has been moving its range northward and is now the number one destroyer of canvasback nests in southern Manitoba. In all likelihood, a considerable number of incubating canvasback hens are killed by this nocturnal predator. Another important factor is that the canvasbacks' preferred wintertime food, wild celery, has been almost totally wiped out along Chesapeake Bay by pollution.

The black duck, once the common duck of the Atlantic flyway, has likewise been losing out since the 1950s. Considered the wariest, quickest, and most alert of all ducks, this cousin of the mallard nests around inland lakes, beaver ponds, and marshes of the northeastern United States and eastern Canada. One reason for its decline is that it readily hybridizes with the mallard, which has been expanding its range eastward. Gradually the black ducks are becoming mallards.

The decline of the adaptable mallard is more difficult to explain. Even the biologists are baffled. This common duck nests just about anywhere, from hayfields to old hawk nests. Their most important nesting grounds, though, are on the mixed prairies of southern Saskatchewan. Many mallards winter in the lower Mississippi Valley and the coastal marshes of Louisiana. The buff-and-brown female mallard does the talking. Her loud, raucous "quack! quack! quack!" is a common marshland sound in the fall. The drake's call is much more subdued, a soft "quack." The female's call of three or more quacks always means to high-flying ducks that all is well and it's safe to come down. This is the call imitated by duck hunters up and down the flyways. Some can do it fairly well; the majority can't.

The blue-winged teal are among the first to leave the northern nesting areas. They start south in late summer, and their numbers reach a peak in late September.

In October, the flights gather momentum: great flocks of geese (Canadas, snow, and white-fronted; brant along the East and West Coasts), ducks (redheads, canvasbacks, scaup, blacks, pintails, and mallards), plus a host of other species.

The migration peaks around mid-November when the northern water becomes icebound. If the freeze-up comes with a storm, a tremendous flight of ducks may occur, especially in the Mississippi and Central flyways, as the birds rush south ahead of the blizzard.

One such storm was the Armistice Day Blizzard of 1940. This storm overtook a main waterfowl migration over the Midwest and forced countless ducks down wherever they could find shelter—on creeks, ponds, sloughs, and rivers. Many duck hunters were also caught unexpectedly by the blizzard. Along the upper Mississippi and Illinois rivers, at least eighty-five hunters died the afternoon and night of the storm.

One day in November 1985 there was a spectacular flight of tundra (whistling) swans through this area. Thousands must have passed that day. The big white swans were flying into a strong crosswind that forced them to fly at lower altitudes than usual, which gave many people an excellent opportunity for a good look at these majestic birds. One flock passed low overhead in the late afternoon following a rain. The strong wind scattered them, and as they struggled to regain formation to the east of us, against the dark-blue background of storm clouds the white swans looked like a string of pearls being gently waved by an invisible hand.

As November draws to a close, most of the waterfowl that survived the perils of migration and the guns of hunters will have their feet in the warmer waters of southern states.

We wish them well. What if, as Aldo Leopold wrote, there were "no more whistling of swift wings when the morning star pales in the east?"

A Tall Oak

A year ago this spring we noticed that one white oak in our woods didn't leaf out with the others. A bit later some of its lower branches grew leaves until they were about the size of a squirrel's foot, then withered and died. One small branch kept its leaves until autumn, but I knew the tree hadn't received enough nourishment to live out the winter. This spring no green appeared. The oak was dead.

We let the great oak season through the spring and summer, and then last week we took wedges, sledges, and saws to lay it to the ground. Since our chain saw barely reached half way across the base of the tree, we sharpened our long-unused six-foot crosscut. The idea conjuring in my mind was for the veteran oak to succumb to the muscle and rhythm of two good sawyers.

After determining where we wanted the tree to drop, between a straight young red oak on the right and a colorful sugar maple on the left, I gamely proceeded to cut the notch. (With the power saw, of course.) Grandpa suggested, since the tree leaned a little, that I saw in from each side just behind the notch and then cut toward the tree's backside, thus keeping the oak from splitting when it went down.

After sawing about three-quarters of the way through, I decided the time was at hand for the crosscut. But alas, after some minutes of strenuous effort, we had to admit that, for us, the skill or art of crosscut sawing had been lost with the past generation. Back to the power saw. With the family well out of harm's way, but close enough to voice their concern, I proceeded much more gingerly, somewhat like a chickadee coming to the sunflower feeder for the first time—skittishly. I'd cut, then stop and look at the top of the tree. Then, suddenly, the saw kerf widened. Quickly shutting off the engine so that no unnatural sound would mar the event, I jumped back. Slowly at first, then rapidly gaining speed, the tree, missing the red oak and pruning the maple, fell with an earthshaking crash.

As the sound died out, I turned to see several of the children with their hands over their ears. I didn't blame them. There is something just plain scary about a big tree falling to earth. The creatures of the woods were silent, and even the dog, who had been barking at a treed squirrel, was quiet.

Gathering around the enormous stump, we started counting the growth rings and calling out birthdays. Three of the children were in the twelve rings of sapwood. When reaching the eighty-second ring we marked it—Grandpa's birth year. All told we counted 311 growth rings, give or take a few years. What had taken nature more than three centuries to make we had undone in about fifteen minutes. Not completely, for there was still a lot of wood to be sawed and burned. But for the first time since the late seventeenth century this space in our woods was now open sky.

Let's suppose that sometime in the fall of 1675 a squirrel buried a white oak acorn. As squirrels usually do, the diligent animal likely cached more nuts than it needed. Or perhaps the squirrel wasn't around to dig out the acorn. It may have been roasted on a spit over an open fire by a band of warriors or hunting Indians. (During that time this part of Ohio had no resident Indian tribes. The Eries, or Cat Nation, of northern Ohio, had been completely destroyed by the Iroquois, a powerful confederacy of tribes from New York and Canada, several decades before. It wasn't until 1750, when the Delawares moved into the Muskingum Valley, that Indians again lived around here.) Meanwhile, this particular acorn remained in the fertile soil to sprout the following spring.

In the 112 years until 1787 and the writing of the Constitution in Philadelphia, the oak grew to only eleven inches in diameter. And then the tree entered a famine of fifty years. In this time the growth rings are so close together that they are almost impossible to count without a magnifying glass. When twenty-one-year-old Jonas Stutzman, the first Amish settler in our county, roamed through here in search of good land in 1809, the oak was struggling for survival. The pioneer may not have noticed the young tree, but surely he would have paid attention to the towering giants that were shading out "our oak."

Then around 1836 or '37 the famine ended. Maybe the pioneer settler cut nearby trees, which I doubt, because they had all the wood they needed from clearing the fields, but more likely several competing neighbor trees died or were blown down in a storm. The growth rings now widened, and in 1875, during the presidency of U. S. Grant, the oak celebrated its two-hundredth birthday and measured seventeen inches across.

The oak probably had, at times, flocks of passenger pigeons feeding on the bounty of acorns in its crown. Finally, no more pigeons appeared, and between the time the last pigeon died in 1914 and 1918 when my grandfather bought the farm, the oak began a period of tremendous growth. It was now the dominant tree in its part of the woods. With its massive root system the well-established tree flourished, even through the drought years of the 1930s. There is no indication of these dry years in the growth rings. In fact, in some of these years the rings were one-quarter-inch wide. The oak continued growing normally until it died. We have no way of knowing the reason for its death. Since it wasn't, to our knowledge, struck by lightning, my guess is that it died of old age.

The good oak will continue to warm our lives in the years to come. The boards sawn from its sturdy trunk will be used around the farm, and the firewood from its many limbs will warm us to the marrow on the cold winter days and long nights.

John Donne began one of his seventeenth-century sermons by saying that: "The ashes of an oak in the chimney are no epitaph of that oak, to tell me how high or how large it was: it tells me not what flocks it sheltered while it stood; nor what men it hurt when it fell."

As I scatter the ashes of our oak across the gardens and fields, I believe I knew this oak intimately. Though I was acquainted with the oak only, you might say, through its twilight years, I know how high and how large it was. I saw my first Blackburnian warbler feeding high among its new leaves one May day many springs ago, and I know that no men were hurt when it fell.

The Beauty of Wood

We didn't get enough firewood cut last year to keep us through this coming winter season. The past winter was mild and "open." Not much snow fell, and the ground stayed muddy instead of freezing. For some reason, I can't get excited about making wood in the mud. We do have an ash we cut and two windfallen trees, a large wild cherry and an old beech, that seasoned through the dry summer and are now ready to be split and stacked.

From any angle you look at it, October is a fine time to be working in the woods. It is in the midst of the most beautiful time of our northern autumn, the time between the green fullness of summer and the barrenness of winter. Working in the chill of a golden autumn morning, one has a sense of time standing still. The week after week of summer's sweltering heat is fading in memory, and winter still seems far away. As the sun climbs into the cloudless sky and I'm swinging the splitting maul, Henry Thoreau's words ring true, "Wood heats you twice, once when you cut it and again when you burn it."

I consider it a privilege to work with wood. Cutting, splitting, and hauling it to the house usually involve all members of the family at one time or another. Many people don't have this opportunity. When the first fire is built on a cool fall evening, and we watch the flames dancing in the firebox and hear the crackling of the stovepipe as it snaps to attention, we know where the heat comes from.

We do not go out of our way to "manage" our woodlot for timber or for firewood. We let it grow naturally, with a little help from us here and there. The woods was never logged-out. Trees were cut only when needed for lumber on the farm. Thus there still are quite a few centuries-old oaks, beeches, and other hardwoods scattered throughout.

"Wolf trees," the state forester called these old beeches when we walked through the woods six years ago, at the time we fenced out the livestock. "Good for very little and should be cut for firewood," he added, "for they shade out more desirable trees."

As we walked I wondered whether the squirrels and red-headed woodpeckers and all the other wild creatures that feed on the abundant beechnuts in October would agree with the forester's appraisal. I thought of all the barns in the neighborhood that have some good solid beech wood in their framing. And besides, few trees are nicer to look at than a beech.

Instead of cutting the beeches to allow sunlight to stimulate new growth, we worked on thinning the stands of ironwoods. Whenever a tall and spreading oak was cut and left an opening in the woods, the scaly-barked ironwoods (American hop-hornbeam) sprouted and thrived in spite of the grazing. (The smooth-barked American hornbeam, or blue beech, is also sometimes called ironwood.) Many of these tough trees are now six to eight inches across and over thirty feet high and shade out the other young hardwoods. We discovered that if an ironwood is girdled with an axe or saw, it will die the second spring and by that fall be dry and ready to burn. Fine-grained and heavy, it is among the finest of firewoods, comparable to coal. Several of these logs will easily hold a fire for twelve to fourteen hours. Every winter I try to girdle maybe three-fourths of the ironwoods in openings left by the oaks, so that by the following autumn we have some ironwood to add to our other fuelwood.

It is amazing how quickly new growth shoots up where openings are made in the woods. White and red oaks, sugar and red maples, hickories and other soft and hardwoods, along with berry brambles, soon form dense thickets, which, of course, are attractive to wildlife. Deer browse and bed in the cover, and last spring a Kentucky warbler was heard singing his rollicking song from a patch of new trees and thorns. After a long game of hide-and-seek we saw the dapper bird, new to our farm, flitting low through the blackberry canes.

The ironwoods are the only live trees, save for some ashes and wild cherries along the woods' edge which were shading the neighbor's field, that we cut for firewood. As a rule, the dead, diseased, and blown-down trees supply us with enough fuel for heating our house, around five to six cords a year. A cord of wood measures four feet by four feet by eight feet. It is said that an acre of woodland will produce about a cord of wood a year indefinitely.

We never try to take out all the dead trees because they are so vital to cavity-nesting birds. Sixteen species of native birds have nested in holes excavated in dead trees and limbs in our woods, from the wood duck and screech owl using a second-hand home excavated by the pileated woodpecker, to the tiny Carolina chickadee and house wren raising their families in former residences of the downy woodpecker. Dead trees are an important part of a natural woodlot.

The American (white) elms, which are dying from Dutch elm disease, are exceptionally good trees for hole-nesting birds, while making only mediocre firewood. The white elms are left standing for the birds. The slippery (red) elms are an entirely different story. They also succumb to the deadly disease but are so hard when dead that woodpeckers cannot drill holes into their reddish wood. And unlike the white elm, red elm makes superb firewood, rock hard, straight grained, and easy to split. The poet must not have had dead red elm in mind when writing:

> Elmwood burns like churchyard mould,
> E'en the very flames are cold.
> Poplar gives a bitter smoke,
> Fills your eyes and makes you choke.
> Apple-wood will scent your room
> With an incense-like perfume.
> But ash wet or ash dry
> For a queen to warm her slippers by.

Of all the different woods we have burned, white ash ranks near or at the top of the list of good wood. It is a beautiful wood to work with and look at—its grains straight and white, an absolute pleasure to split, and clean to handle. While maybe not quite as good as red elm, ash does give a lot of heat, burning clean and leaving very little ash. Definitely a wood to warm your feet by. (Incidentally, a cord of good seasoned hardwood, which is equal to a ton of coal, will leave about sixty pounds of ashes, while the ton of coal will produce from two hundred to three hundred pounds of ashes.)

Last winter I was sawing up and splitting an ash log that was partly hollow. At times cracks opened in the split wood, exposing black carpenter ants and their eggs. Some of the insects and the eggs remained in the wood, while others rolled to the ground. After splitting maybe half a cord, I set down the maul and sat on the log to rest before stacking the wood. It wasn't long until a chickadee came and perched on a stick of wood, cocked its head to the side, and snatched an ant egg. Soon several of its friends appeared and helped search for and feast on the ant eggs, which must be a chickadee delicacy. It was a two-way deal: by my work I made the eggs available to the chickadees; now while I rested, the little birds entertained me with their antics and friendliness. After a while, their appetites sated, the chickadees moved on down the hill, and I stacked the wood.

Apple is considered an aromatic wood, though when we burn it I can never detect any "incense-like perfume." Sassafras and hickory, however, will give off delightful aromas that scent the room.

Over the years I often pondered why the lovely tree, whose white flowers in the spring are symbolic of the crucifixion, is named the dogwood. A few years ago we discovered the reason. A dogwood tree died, and we cut it up and stacked the wood on the porch along with the ash and other wood. Sometime in the winter, when the wood was slightly wet from blowing snow, we stacked a pile by the stove to dry before burning. At the supper table one of the children suddenly remarked, "I smell a dog!" No, I couldn't. Some of the others thought they did, too. Following their noses, they ended up at the wood barrel. When they called me, they were holding a piece of wood that smelled like a hound drying by the fire after a night of hunting in the rain. It was dogwood.

The economic advantages of heating with your own wood over coal are obvious. By burning wood, we save five tons of coal from being strip-mined, a practice that adds little to the local economy. Our cost for a year's supply of wood runs around thirty dollars, not counting the depreciation on the chain saw, which is so old it quit losing value some time back. Every fall, the local engine shop has a sale on saw chains at which you buy one and get a second one for a dollar or two. This lowers the cost of saw maintenance to near insignificance. And my labor is free. On the other hand, watching the chickadees eat ant eggs was worth at least ten dollars a minute. Even if you buy your wood, you can be sure the money goes directly to some hard-working person for his labor, instead of to the coal company which would buy more earth-ripping machinery.

The cost savings are only a part of the pleasures of wood burning. To me, being warmed on a cold winter evening by the glowing embers of good wood is for some reason more satisfying than turning up a thermostat.

Autumn Colors

Autumn's clear cool days and crisp mornings, with Orion, the mighty hunter, high in the early southern sky, rekindle memories of barefoot days when we brought home the cows, shuffling our feet for a few moments in the warmth where the gentle creatures had lain. Then I loved the colors of October, and I still do. First come the reds of the Virginia creeper's scarlet leaves and the glossy scarlet of the black gum. Later in the month we have the red maples, scarlet oaks, and dogwoods; and then the reddish orange of bittersweet, and, finest of all, the sugar maples. Add to this spectrum the bright yellow of the aspens and tulip poplars, the yellowish brown to bluish purple of the ashes, and the green to burgundy and purple of the mighty oaks.

Many believe that a hard frost is needed to bring out the best colors on the hardwoods. Actually, it is now known that an early killing frost hurts rather than helps the coloring process. A lot of sunshine, not frost, is needed to bring about the most spectacular display of autumn colors.

The coloring process begins in late summer and early fall when shorter days prompt the trees to begin withdrawing sap into their trunks and roots for the coming winter. The circulation to the leaves is thus cut off, and the green, which is the chlorophyll, begins to fade, revealing the vivid gold, yellow, and orange that were present all along but were hidden by chlorophyll during the summer months. Some people think that the sugars sealed in the autumn leaves oxidize, producing the varied hues of reds, blues, and purples. If an early frost interrupts this process, the leaves may never reach their expected brilliance and will instead appear drab and sear. Then we often say the fall was too wet or too dry or the frosts were too late. In other words, we still don't understand many of the mysteries of nature.

Autumn's colors are only a part of its appeal. It is also a good time for observing wildlife in its peak condition and for nut gathering. We usually find time for both.

Last year I took half a day to gather a pail of hickory nuts, taking the long way through the woods so that I'd end up along a fencerow where I knew I'd find several shellbark hickory trees that usually produce large nuts with extra-sweet kernels.

I hadn't even entered the woods when I noticed the first wildlife sign of the season. On the ground, about four feet or so beneath a drooping limb of wild cherry, was a bare, scraped patch of earth. The patch was about three feet across and had several white-tailed deer tracks in it. Examining the twigs on the limb overhead, I noticed that several were broken—obviously the work of a white-tailed buck marking his territory, a sort of business card in the world of the deer. A little ways down from the scrape was a sapling two inches thick whose bark had been stripped away, exposing the white sapwood. Here the buck had rubbed his antlers, maybe to remove the summer's velvet—but since it appeared quite fresh, my guess is that the little maple served as an imagined rival for the benefit of two does in the vicinity.

Entering the woods, I soon found an old log to sit on. Resting and watching I could feel the rhythm of the season. The trees were alive with migrating yellow-rumped warblers and our resident birds who were busily feeding. The birds also seemed to be enjoying the splendid day. From a distance, a fox squirrel started working my way and then became suspicious and scurried up a nearby oak. Suddenly there was a swoosh of wings as a hawk dived at the squirrel and missed, by a hair. The raptor lit on a branch hardly twenty feet from me to appraise the situation. Slowly I turned my head to look into the glaring red eyes of a Cooper's hawk. The hunter turned its attention back to the hunted, who was jerking its bushy tail in a silent scold. The hawk, with hackles raised, again swooped at the squirrel and again missed, then continued on through the woods in search of an easier meal. After what seemed like a long silence, the songbirds resumed their feeding. The squirrel got in the last word. From a crotch high in the oak it scolded, long and loud.

My presence in the woods didn't go unnoticed. In the safety of a broken and hollow beech a great horned owl grew uneasy and then, on broad wings, took flight for the supposed safety of the far end of the woods. But there the big bird was greeted by a pair of crows who soon called in all their crow neighbors. If I understood crow language, I'm sure I'd have heard some unkind words directed at the owl.

Leaving the raucous crows behind, I left the woods and walked along the fencerow. Here and there a few asters and goldenrods were still in bloom. A bumblebee buzzed loudly from flower to flower. Was this a queen bumblebee seeking food before finding a safe, warm place for the winter? Or was it a worker bee on a last flight before succumbing to the cold? I couldn't tell.

I passed a stretch of sassafras trees, and hanging like tiny pendulums from some of the twigs were the cocoons of promethea moths. Within the silken shell, the larva of this pretty moth would live out the winter. Unless a downy woodpecker decided otherwise.

Shortly after I arrived at the shellbark hickories, my pail was filled to the brim with fallen nuts. The hickories, like the walnut trees, had already lost most of their leaves.

I checked and cleaned out several bluebird houses, making

sure the deer mice had settled in the woodpile and not in the birdhouses, and I then headed across the fields for home.

I can't help but feel somewhat melancholy as autumn draws to a close. A time so abundantly beautiful can't last forever. As Wendell Berry so eloquently writes in a poem about October:

> Now constantly there is the sound,
> quieter than rain,
> of leaves falling.

> Under their loosening bright
> gold, the sycamore limbs
> bleach whiter.

> Now the only flowers
> are beeweed and aster, spray
> of their white and lavender
> over the brown leaves.

> The calling of a crow sounds
> loud—a landmark—now
> that the life of summer falls
> silent, and the nights grow.

Woodland Gold

Once a friend and I were on a nature walk with our teacher, who suddenly stopped, expressing surprise. No matter how much we badgered him to tell us what he saw, he refused to reveal his discovery. As we continued through the early autumn woods, most of us soon forgot the incident. One upper-grade boy, however, did not forget. Over the next several years, his thoughts would on occasion return to that walk and its unusual episode. Finally, on a hunch, he returned to the spot and found what he had suspected—a patch of wild ginseng.

Ginseng has intrigued the imagination of the American people ever since it was discovered near Montreal in 1716 by Joseph Lafitau, a French Jesuit missionary. The interest, though, is mainly in the high prices some Oriental countries are willing to pay for the roots. With dried ginseng root bringing up to sixty dollars a pound at the time, our schoolteacher well knew that to divulge the whereabouts of ginseng to a bunch of schoolboys wasn't in the best interests of the rare plant.

American ginseng (*Panax quinquefolium*) is a small plant, ranging from ten to twenty inches in height when mature. The name comes from the Chinese *jen-shen*, which means "man-shape." The root often has a trunk and extremities somewhat like arms and legs, and thus resembles the human form. The plant likes rich, cool woods. It often grows on gentle north slopes and other spots with well-drained soils and is found across the eastern half of North America from Quebec to Manitoba, and south to Arkansas and Georgia. A ginseng plant may take as long as eighteen months to germinate and another three to six years to reach maturity.

The plant begins with two leaves, each with five lobes, three large lobes on the front of the stem and two smaller ones in the back. It is sometimes called five-fingers for its five-fingered leaf, hence the specific name *quinquefolium*. As it matures, more leaves are added. By the third summer, it may flower and bear a cluster of small green berries which contain the seeds. The berries ripen to a scarlet-red in September.

The Chinese, especially, have for thousands of years extolled the merits of ginseng as a medicinal plant. Five hundred years before the birth of Christ, Confucius wrote about the healing powers of the plant. In the sixteenth century Li-Shih-chen, Chinese physician-naturalist, praised ginseng as "a tonic to the five viscera, quieting animal spirits, establishing the soul, allaying fear, expelling evil effluvia, brightening the eye, opening up the heart, benefiting the understanding, and, if taken for some time, it will invigorate the body and prolong life." If ginseng does all this it's no wonder that the Chinese have long considered it to be "the queen of medicinal herbs."

Soon after word of the plant's powers spread from the Orient to Europe and the French discovered it in Canada, American colonists were finding ginseng from New England to the southern Appalachians. It is thought that some settlers learned of the plant's medicinal values from the Indians, who not only used the roots as a tea to ward off fatigue and treat illness but also as an aphrodisiac.

By the late 1700s the boom in the ginseng trade with the Far East began. Soon Indians and white settlers alike were combing the forests for the increasingly valuable roots. In 1784 George Washington, visiting his land holdings west of the Appalachians along the Kanawah River, recorded in his diary that "passing over the Mountains I met numbers of Persons and Pack horses going east with Ginseng."

Several years later on September 22, 1787, John Matthews, a surveyor for the Ohio Land Company, wrote: "Left our camp at sunrise and moved about five miles to the west and encamped about half a mile to the east of the dividing ridge between the waters of the Muskingum and Short creek. Here we dug ginseng until Thursday, 27th. It grew here in great abundance. Men accustomed to the work could dig from forty to sixty pounds a day. The roots were generally very large. The biggest grow where the land is very rich and open to the sun. Many roots of ginseng of a medium size appear to be twenty to thirty years old, which is ascertained by the number of points, or scars, on top of the root, every year producing one. But I found roots of a good size not more than three or four years old." It has been claimed that the men of the Ohio Land Company spent more time digging 'seng than they did surveying the land.

The boom couldn't last. After two centuries, the overharvesting of the root began to take its toll. In addition, by the end of the 1800s, the hardwood forests had been gutted to the point where they could no longer supply the demand for wild ginseng in China. At this time some farsighted people saw what was happening and started to cultivate the prized plants. It has been estimated that at the turn of the century as many as ten thousand farmers were raising ginseng. Many suffered financial ruin when a fungus blight attacked the crops in 1904. A few stayed in the business, burning brushpiles to kill the fungus in the soil where they then started new seedlings. Eventually, other methods were developed to combat the blight, and to this day a considerable amount of ginseng is cultivated for export. Ironically, the ginseng available at local health food stores is usually imported from Korea.

Although the medical profession in the United States was slow in crediting ginseng with any medicinal value, there were individuals outside the profession who fervently believed in its powers. An early colonist wrote: "The Root of this is of wonderful Vertue in many Cases, particularly to raise the Spirits and promote Perspiration, which makes it a Specifick in Colds and Coughs. I carry'd home this Treasure, with as much Joy, as if every Root had been the Graft of the Tree of Life, and washt and dry'd it carefully."

One physician who did believe in the plant's healing properties was the late Dr. Arthur R. Harding of Columbus, Ohio. Dr. Harding devoted his life to cultivating ginseng and experimenting with it on his patients. In his book *Ginseng and Other Medicinal Plants*, Dr. Harding observed that ginseng root medication had "cured every case where I have used it with one exception and that was a case of consumption in its last stages." (Dr. A. R. Harding was also the founder and long-time publisher of *Fur—Fish—Game* magazine.)

Even though ginseng is rare and may be endangered in some states, it can still be found growing wild. I found my first plant purely by chance. I was in my early teens and had taken the morning off to pursue squirrels. I entered the woods and eased around a towering white oak. As I waited for my eyes to become accustomed to the darkness of the woods, something red caught my eye. There in front of me was a ginseng plant with a clump of red berries. It was what ginseng hunters call a four-pronger, and it seemed to me to be almost three feet tall. Of course, it wasn't. About a week later I returned to admire my find, only to discover that it was gone! Somebody had found it and dug out the root.

I didn't find any more ginseng until about six years ago when a friend and I stumbled upon some. This time, there were many more plants—perhaps several dozen. My friend is as protective of our patch of ginseng as a mother hen is of her chicks. Every fall he picks the berries as soon as they ripen and spreads them about, covering them with a bit of leaf litter. Thus the plants are much more difficult to find. Last fall he counted close to seventy-five seed-bearing plants. Our hope is that they won't be discovered by a "digger."

Maybe some day we'll dig some of the roots for our own use. But for now we're content to visit the ginseng, sit and stroll through its midst, and ponder the mystery surrounding its curious root.

The Return
of a Native

It was almost dark as we rounded the point of woods jutting into the lake and entered the small bay. We stopped paddling at the sight of a V-shaped ripple and waited motionless, hardly daring to breathe. In the gathering dusk the only sound we could hear was the dripping of water from our upraised paddles onto the mirrorlike surface of the lake. When the creature making the ripple was about twenty feet from the canoe, it stopped—then crack! The beaver slapped its tail down hard on the water and dived in alarm, for man is its greatest enemy. Although I had seen beavers a few times previously, never before had I heard them slap their warning of danger. I was astonished at its loudness.

The beaver is North America's largest rodent and is the only animal that alters its environment to suit its needs. This it does sometimes to the consternation of farmers and fishermen, who complain of flooded fields and dammed trout streams. Likewise, in the Southeast, lumbermen blame the beaver for flooding valuable stands of commercial timber. But aside from a few such complaints, the beaver has many qualities that endear it to people: it mates for life and lives as a family unit, it is clean and gentle, and it loves hard work.

The industrious rodent is justified in fearing man because it has been trapped and hunted for centuries. No other animal has prompted the exploration of an entire continent as the beaver did in North America. Beginning in the early 1600s, trappers wandered from the Atlantic to the Pacific in quest of the beaver's luxurious pelt for European markets. Very few beaver survived this era. John Madson writes in his book *Where the Sky Began*, "For two hundred years the French *coureurs de bois*, with the help of Indians, had hunted and trapped in the heart of the tall prairie. By the time the early settlers arrived in Iowa, most of the otter and beaver had vanished down trade routes that were old before the first covered wagons appeared."

Following the French and Indian War, when France gave its rights east of the Mississippi to England, the Hudson's Bay Company, which was chartered in 1670, controlled the fur trade in the East. Meanwhile, the North West Company of Montreal was developing the trade in the West. Its domain reached all the way to the Arctic in the north, the Big Bend of the Missouri River to the south, and west to the Rockies. It was primarily the threat of the North West Company that prompted President Thomas Jefferson to send explorers Lewis and Clark on their expedition up the Missouri River. Jefferson's goal was to find a better passage to the Pacific Northwest, thus enabling the United States to capture the Northwestern beaver trade from Canada.

While the United States was seeking an easier route to the Northwest, the North West Company of Montreal relied upon voyagers to transport their goods across wild and treacherous Canadian rivers. "These French Canadians," writes Sigurd Olson, "lived and traveled with a spirit, sense of adventure and pride in their calling that balanced its enormous distances and hardships. These wiry little men—seldom more than five feet four or five—dressed in breech cloth, moccasins and leather leggings reaching to the thighs, a belted shirt topped off with a red cap and feather. From dawn until dark they paddled their great canoes and packed enormous loads, facing storms, wild uncharted rivers, hostile Indians, and ruthless rivals with a joy and abandon that has possibly never been equaled in man's conquest and exploitation of any new country."

The fur trade peaked in the 1880s. By then the Hudson's Bay Company had taken over the North West Company, and John Jacob Astor's Pacific Fur Company was well established in the West. During the period that the demand for beavers was at its peak, incredible numbers of skins were sold on European markets. Between 1853 and 1877, the Hudson's Bay Company sold nearly three million beaver pelts in London. Profits were often enormous, not only for the traders but also for the trappers. One trapper reportedly earned fifty thousand dollars in a single season. But as the saying goes, all good things come to an end, and so did the era of beaver trapping and trading. By 1900, the beaver in North America, whose population has been estimated to have been sixty million before the arrival of the first Europeans, was nearly extinct.

A few isolated colonies managed to survive, and these continued their ways unchanged. The beaver is remarkably well adapted to life in the water. When it dives, valves automatically close its ears and nose while loose flaps of skin seal off the mouth behind its four chisel-edged cutting teeth. This enables it to carry and gnaw branches under water. In addition, unusually large lungs and liver allow it to remain submerged for up to fifteen minutes.

A colony typically consists of eight to ten beavers—two adults plus their offspring of two years. A beaver is considered full grown when it weighs between forty and sixty pounds. They differ from most mammals, however, in that they never stop growing. The largest one on record was trapped sixty years ago in northern Wisconsin. It weighed 110 pounds.

When the two to five young, called kits, are born in May or June, the two-year-olds are driven away from the colony by the parents. The evicted young then begin their search for a new home. When suitable habitat is found, they immediately set to work building a dam. The dam is made up chiefly of small sticks and mud mixed with a few rocks or whatever is readily available. If the dam is near civilization, this can mean discarded cans and bottles, old tennis shoes, and even car tires. The upstream surface is smoothly plastered with mud, and the dams can vary from ten feet or less to hundreds of feet in length. As the water fills in behind the dam the beavers start building their lodge, which will be their home and their assurance of survival during the long winter months. It too is constructed of sticks and mud and is around twelve feet in diameter with three to six feet visible above the water. The two to five entrances are always underwater. The story is told of how mountainman John Colter, in the Yellowstone Country, escaped a pursuing band of Blackfeet Indians by diving into a beaver pond and coming up inside one of their lodges.

With the completion of the lodge, the beavers waste no time in storing enough food to last through the winter. Although softwoods like cottonwood, aspen, and soft maple are their preferred fare, they will, if necessity demands it, eat many other plants, including corn. The cache of food is stored underwater next to the lodge for easy under-ice access. Beavers are frugal and waste little food. This became clear several years ago when I came upon a freshly gnawed aspen stump that must have been ten inches in diameter. All that remained of the thirty-foot tree were neat heaps of chips spaced every two to three feet apart, indicating the length of logs the beavers carried away. Toward the upper end of the tree where the wood became more manageable, the distance between piles of chips lengthened to four to six feet. Amazingly, nothing was wasted; even the tiniest twig was carried to their winter food cache.

As the colony grows, all members, except the small kits, help in keeping the dam repaired. I once opened a small area in a dam, and by the following morning the breach had been repaired. Beavers know well that the life of the colony depends on the dam.

Not only the beavers benefit from a new dam, but their industry provides a new environment for many different species of wildlife. As cattails sprout in the backwaters, muskrats move in and build their miniature lodges. Also finding the new beaver pond to their liking are wood, mallard, and black ducks, fish, turtles, and frogs, and great blue herons in search of frogs. Rails, marsh wrens, and swamp sparrows move in, and after a year or two, the prothonotary warblers will nest in hollow snags of trees that died from the flooding.

At the turn of the century, as people became aware of the beaver's plight, several states passed laws to protect the few animals that remained. In 1906 New York imported fourteen beavers from Yellowstone National Park, and in a little over a decade these had increased to several thousand. Other states followed New York's example and the beaver has made a remarkable recovery. It is estimated that there are six to twelve million beaver in North America at present. Wildlife managers caution, however, that such figures don't mean very much. When taking a census, experts make the assumption that each lodge contains five to seven beavers. This is guessing at best. A friend of mine owns a marsh that had what he thought to be a colony of beavers. As he related the story to me, "Since a lot of trees were being cut down, I decided to trap just one of the tree cutters. And you know, when I caught that one, a big male, all the work stopped. The dam deteriorated for want of repairs and there was no beaver activity at all. My supposed colony was home to simply one old bachelor beaver. To imagine he was doing all that work himself! I was sorry I trapped him."

Beaver numbers have increased to the point that they are again being trapped and their pelts used by the fur industry for coats, jackets, and black "wool" hats. More than two hundred thousand are trapped annually.

Two years ago some neighbor boys were on their way to our farm to hunt rats and house sparrows for the school's pest hunt. While crossing the bridge below our house, they heard a splash in the water. Suspecting a coon, they were surprised when the beams of their flashlights revealed a good-sized beaver. They quickly ran to tell us, and then several of our children and our dog were also able to get a good look at the traveling engineer. It was milking time, so I missed seeing it, but just knowing that the beaver had swum and walked across half a mile of our farm, after an absence of possibly two hundred years, was reward enough.

Autumn
Hawk Flights

It is a glorious October day. A fresh northwesterly breeze ripples across the ripening corn. As the warm sun strikes the earth and heats the air next to the ground, the air rises, creating a thermal. Soaring and wheeling in this upward current of heated air is the first hawk of the day, a redtail.

The sailing hawk, we suppose at first, is likely one of the pair of redtails that nested in our neighbor's woods, or one of the two young they raised. However, at this time of the year, it is more likely a migrating hawk loafing its way south for the winter.

Even though our farm is not in a geographical hotspot for migrating hawks, we do see fair numbers every fall. From early September through December, it is possible to spot a variety of hawks, ranging from the early broad-winged to the late rough-legged. There are a number of locations in eastern North America, though, that are bottlenecks where thousands of hawks might pass in a single day.

Two of the most notable spots where natural barriers funnel the migrating birds through one area are Hawk Mountain in eastern Pennsylvania and Duluth, Minnesota, on the western-most point of Lake Superior.

Set in the Blue Mountains of eastern Pennsylvania, the Kittatinny Ridge forms the southeastern edge of the Appalachian chain. Originating in New York, the ridge runs virtually unbroken across northern New Jersey and eastern Pennsylvania, all the way to Maryland.

As autumn approaches, the hawks leave their summer haunts in eastern Canada and New England and move toward the south. While many follow the Atlantic coastline, large numbers, especially the soaring hawks, stay inland and follow the Appalachians. With the rising heat and the autumn winds rebounding off the mountains and providing the lift needed for excellent soaring, the migrating hawks can travel great distances with very little effort. The hawks fly from ridge to ridge across the Appalachians until they reach the unbroken Kittatinny which they then follow to the southwest. For the most part, the Kittatinny Ridge is broad, and the hawk flights are spread out, making them hard to follow. But as the ridge nears Hawk Mountain it narrows and rises, and the hawks' line of flight also narrows. It is along this bottleneck of rocky outcroppings that spectacular hawk flights can occur during favorable weather—often following a day of brisk northwest winds in September and October.

Before the founding of Hawk Mountain Sanctuary, the sandstone outcrops were the favorite hiding places for local gunners who lay in wait for the unsuspecting hawks as they passed close to the mountain. Hundreds of hawks would be killed in a single day, and it is estimated that hundreds of thousands of hawks and eagles were slaughtered before the carnage ended in 1934. That year a group of conservation-minded people purchased fourteen hundred acres of the mountain and turned it into a sanctuary for birds of prey.

At Hawk Ridge Nature Reserve in Duluth, Minnesota, even more impressive flights can occasionally be observed than those at Hawk Mountain. The natural barrier in this case isn't a long mountain range but Lake Superior. The hawks that have spent the summer in the boreal woods and prairies of Canada encounter the lake's three-hundred-mile shoreline on their southern journey. Rather than cross the lake they follow its shore in a southwesterly direction until reaching Duluth and the end of the lake before spreading out. From the high bluffs overlooking Lake Superior, on good days hundreds of migrating hawks can be seen flying by, often at eye level or below. One September day in 1962 an estimated 15,600 hawks were seen in the eastern section of Duluth between 9:00 A.M. and 4:00 P.M. Broad-winged and red-tailed hawks were the most numerous, but there were also many sharp-shinned hawks, kestrels (sparrow hawks), peregrine falcons, and goshawks. In addition, flock after flock of flickers and other small birds passed overhead.

Another excellent hawk lookout is at Cape May Point, which is at the extreme southern tip of New Jersey. Hawks following the Atlantic coastline find themselves confronted by the wide expanse of Delaware Bay and congregate at the point before venturing across the open water; they may also turn, following the coast to the northwest where the bay eventually narrows.

A similar situation occurs at Point Pelee, Ontario. Here, too, the hawks assemble and linger before flying across Lake Erie, awarding the lake's north shore with its own spectacular flights, particularly at Hawk Cliffs.

The migration begins in late August and early September with the bald eagles and ospreys on their way to the Gulf Coast. By mid-September, the broad-winged hawks appear, sometimes in immense numbers at the points of concentration. At Hawk Ridge in Duluth, for example, approximately 24,000 broadwings were counted on September 22, 1970. And on September 14, 1979, 21,448 of these small soaring hawks passed Hawk Mountain in Pennsylvania!

During migration the broad-winged hawks mill in swirling flocks called "kettles," somewhat resembling a swarm of bees. Only once have I seen a kettle of broadwings. That was during the spring migration a number of years ago, when we were planting corn. I had taken binoculars along to the field to check out some sparrows, hoping to find a grasshopper sparrow among them, when I happened to turn the binoculars skyward to watch a high-flying hawk. It was a redtail, but beyond it, invisible to the naked eye, were dozens of broad-winged hawks milling around in numerous kettles. They were steadily moving toward the northeast, and the flight continued until late afternoon. I have no way of knowing how many hawks passed overhead that day, but there must have been thousands.

In early October the broadwings give way to the sharp-shinned hawks and their slightly larger cousins, the Cooper's hawks. These shorter-winged, longer-tailed hawks seldom soar like the buteos but fly by alternately flapping and sailing. It's a sharp-shinned if it's "three flaps and a sail, and a long square tail." The similar Cooper's hawk has a rounded tail. The bigger goshawk, also in the same family, is rarely seen in migration. Of all the hawks tallied at Hawk Mountain, the goshawk makes up less than one-half of one percent of the total, compared to the sharp-shinned at 23 percent.

From October through December it's not uncommon to see redtails, northern harriers (formerly called marsh hawks), and kestrels moving south or possibly selecting a winter territory where ample food, primarily the meadow vole, is available. Cooper's hawks sometimes have the unfortunate habit of establishing themselves close to bird feeders. Since they feed on small birds, a well-populated feeder is all they desire. One of these "blue darters" frequented our yard last winter and dined on a junco and several house sparrows before moving farther south as the winter worsened.

Our local population of red-tailed hawks, I tend to think, also migrate south for the winter and are in turn replaced by redtails from northern regions. My reason for believing so is that for the past two winters a partially albino redtail included the eastern part of our farm in its hunting range; when spring came it departed, presumably to its summer range, and was replaced by a pair of redtails.

While the rough-legged hawks travel south from the Arctic and spend the winter with us, the broad-winged hawks and peregrine falcons fly all the way to Central and South America. Many of the other species, though, don't travel beyond the southern coastal states where they then spend the winter.

A lot of us bird-watchers would enjoy a chance to see the king of raptors, the magnificent golden eagle, or the peregrine falcon, during the fall migration. In ancient falconry these two birds were reserved for the nobility. The eagle was restricted to the emperor and the peregrine belonged to the next in rank. The golden eagle I have yet to see, but on one occasion I had the good fortune to see a peregrine. The falcon was flying fairly high when suddenly it dived at a low-flying shorebird. The poor shorebird flew for its life, but it need not have worried because the fleet-winged falcon was only teasing. Through binoculars we could clearly see its pointed wings, black crown, and wedge or "sideburn" extending below its eye. We watched breathlessly until the falcon flew out of sight on its way to South America.

The peregrine falcon is considered to be the swiftest bird on earth, with speeds when diving at prey exceeding 175 miles per hour. Solomon once wrote, "The way of an eagle in the air is too wonderful to understand"; I would include the peregrine as well.

It is good that hawks and eagles are now protected by federal and state laws, and that as the majestic birds wing their way south every autumn, they are greeted with binoculars instead of guns.

October

O sun and skies and clouds of June
And flowers of June together,
Ye cannot rival for one hour
October's bright blue weather.
                    Helen Hunt Jackson
          OCTOBER'S BRIGHT BLUE WEATHER

There is something about October that no other month can match. The brilliant colors of the hardwoods, the crisp morning air spiked with a faint tinge of skunk, the clear skies laced with a few cumulus clouds drifting lazily across it—all these spell October.

Along with October comes a certain sadness because the spring we so eagerly awaited has passed, and so has the summer; now we realize that winter is waiting in the wings. However, this melancholy is soon overwhelmed by the spell of the season as we gather walnuts, hickory nuts, and chestnuts, and hustle to get the corn cribbed.

Though we regret the passing of summer, the time does arrive when we look forward to a killing frost so that we can cease our battles with the lamb's-quarters, pigweeds, and purslane, and hang up our hoes for the year. Most gardeners probably reach this point sometime during the fall. In a few months the new seed catalogs will be arriving in the mail, and our struggles with the weeds will be forgotten. Resolutions will be made to start the melons earlier, and maybe set out the Siberian toma-

toes a week sooner so that we'll have ripe tomatoes by the fourth
of July.

For the small-scale dairy farmer, October is almost perfect.
The cool nights have eliminated the bothersome flies, and the
cows, content on legume pastures, have a desire to produce
large quantities of milk.

Along about the middle of the month we hear a sound that
we've been waiting for—the quacking and gabbling of migrating ducks and geese. Every autumn since 1975 hundreds and
often thousands of migrating waterfowl visit our pond, Levi
D. Miller's, and some other ponds in the area, and linger, feeding on waste grain in the picked cornfields until snow and cold
weather in late November drive them farther south. Though
primarily mallards, there are also a considerable number of
black ducks, American wigeons, and pintails, and a lesser
number of blue- and green-winged teal, shovelers, wood
ducks, lesser scaups, and coots.

We have often wondered why these thousands of wild
ducks, especially the wary black ducks, come to these small
farm ponds, as you could say, in the middle of nowhere.

There may be several reasons. One, the forty-five-hundred-
acre Killbuck Wildlife Area, the largest inland area of swamp
and marshland in Ohio, is only ten miles west of our farm.
This "wasteland" was privately owned until around twelve
years ago when the state began buying it. As the land was purchased, it was opened for public hunting, and then, because of
the heavy hunting pressure, the ducks were forced to seek sanctuary elsewhere.

A second reason is that in the early seventies we had some
semi-wild mallards on our pond and, after several years of
good hatches, we were overstocked. So a friend and I live-
trapped thirty-five and released them in the Killbuck marshes.
A farmer from that area, who was with us when we turned the
ducks loose, told me later that many of the ducks were shot

soon afterward by poachers. Could some of these mallards have survived and then, in the following fall, shown their wild kin the way to our farm for food and protection?

The first ducks begin coming in to the pond the day the duck season opens. For some reason they do not stay on the pond at night, except occasionally during a full moon, but prefer to return to the marshes. They leave the pond about a half hour before dark and return in the morning just after daybreak. Thus their departure and arrival from the marshes are after and before legal shooting hours. And to think that some people call them dumb ducks.

We very seldom feed the ducks because we want them to retain their wild ways, and besides, we like to see them fly. As someone said, "one duck flying is worth ten on the water." It is especially exciting to watch the graceful birds come in when there's a brisk west wind. Since ducks almost always land into the wind, they set their wings and come in over the house. To hear the air rush through their pinion feathers is truly thrilling.

The ducks usually reach peak numbers during the third week in November. After the first significant snow and cold snap, they depart. Where do they go? According to John Latecki, a state game protector, most of the band returns from ducks banded in the Killbuck Wildlife Area have been from Arkansas. So apparently many of the ducks spend the winter months along the lower Mississippi River and in the surrounding wetlands. I'm reminded of the words written by William Cullen Bryant in his poem "To A Waterfowl":

> Thou'rt gone; the abyss of heaven
> Hath swallowed up thy form; yet on my heart
> Deeply hath sunk the lesson thou hast given,
>   And shall not soon depart.

He who from zone to zone
Guides through the boundless sky thy certain flight,
In the long way that I must tread alone
Will lead my steps aright.

Toward the end of October, with the corn harvest in, we have time to walk in the woods, replenish the woodpile, and reflect on the summer's toils and sweat. There's time, too, for giving thanks to the Provider of all things for another bounteous year.

The Adaptable
White-tailed Deer

We both saw the deer at the same time. The animal had crested a hill and then stopped when it saw my dad and me working in the woods below. There, silhouetted against an overcast November sky, was the biggest, most magnificent white-tailed buck we had ever seen. The size of its antlers was incredible; if we had been in the western United States instead of Ohio, I would have thought we were looking at a mule deer. After five, maybe ten seconds, the buck turned and disappeared in the direction from which it had come.

I can't exactly explain why, but the sight of a splendid whitetail never fails to fascinate me. I think it was Aldo Leopold who wrote, "Babes do not tremble when they are shown a golf ball, but I should not like to own the boy whose hair does not lift his hat when he sees his first deer." What is especially rewarding for me is that it is only in the last ten years that we regularly see deer on our farm. They have been absent for perhaps more than a hundred years, and as recently as twenty-five or thirty years ago, if somebody saw one of the shy creatures, people soon heard about it.

The whitetail, when afforded some protection, has adapted to man and civilization remarkably well; so well, in fact, that they're now fairly common in the suburbs of some of our bigger cities. Some wildlife biologists even claim that there are more deer now than there were at the time the first white settlers arrived.

However, there were quite a few deer in Ohio in the early 1800s, according to Henry Howe's "Historical Collections of Ohio": a gang hunt in 1818 that covered one township in Medina county produced three hundred deer, plus seventeen wolves, twenty-one bears, and other game. Ernest Thompson Seton, in one of his books, took the figures of this hunt, times the area of suitable whitetail range, and came up with a population estimate of forty million deer in colonial America. This figure is probably too high, since virgin forest with hardly any undergrowth and no surrounding farmland is not ideal whitetail habitat.

John James Audubon, on a trip through New England in 1833, saw so many white-tailed deer that he wrote, "In that wild and secluded part of the country, the common deer were without number, and it was with great difficulty that we kept our dogs with us." Nonetheless, with the settlers' year-round taste for venison, and relentless hunting with dogs, snares, and guns, by the late 1800s the deer in Ohio and throughout parts of the eastern United States were virtually extinct. Finally, under public pressure, laws were passed banning market hunting, and in Ohio, deer hunting was prohibited for over forty years.

The game management people like to point to the white-tailed deer herd as one of their truly successful efforts. Of course, their limited stocking of deer in the '20s and '30s, along with strict game law enforcement, helped the deer, but a natural occurrence likely did more than their efforts to promote the whitetail's comeback.

During the late 1920s and throughout the '30s, because of topsoil lost to poor farming practices and the economic crunch of the Great Depression, thousands of hill farms in southeastern Ohio and other marginal farming regions in the East and Midwest were abandoned. As these farms reverted to forest, they provided excellent range for the deer. Also consider that since deer are ruminants, subject to the same diseases as cattle, they benefited indirectly from vaccinations developed at about this time for beef and dairy herds, which all but eradicated brucellosis (Bang's disease) and leptospirosis, two highly contagious and devastating diseases which cause reproductive failure and often sterility in afflicted animals. Because of the extermination of the large predators such as wolves and mountain lions, the conditions were excellent for deer, and the astonishingly fertile whitetail began to recover. Biologists say that two dozen does have the potential of producing three thousand descendants in ten years.

In 1943 Ohio opened three counties to deer hunting, and 8,500 hunters bagged 168 deer, for a success ratio of one deer for every 50 hunters. By 1973 hunting was allowed in 59 counties, where 108,000 hunters harvested 7,500, for a success ratio of 1 in 14. In 1983, all 88 counties were open on hunting, and 265,000 hunters bagged 59,000 whitetails, for a hunter success ratio of 1 in 4.4.

Now it seems that the Division of Wildlife wants to undo all that it has accomplished, for this year the season is open to both sexes, including fawns, in most of Ohio's counties. The claim is that it's almost impossible to overhunt white-tailed deer. Though the whitetail can take care of its hide remarkably well, it can be overhunted, especially in wooded areas interspersed with farmland. This has happened in southern Maine, where last fall, for the first time in the state's history, there was a bucks-only season, a sure sign of a declining deer herd.

Maybe I'm too pessimistic about our state's permissive deer season; now that we frequently see deer about the farm we'd regret to see their numbers decline. But their ability to survive is amazing. This is especially true of the older bucks that have survived several hunting seasons.

Two years ago, on the last day of the gun season, we were at the supper table when I happened to see my neighbor walking down the road on his way home from hunting. I went out on the porch to ask him if he had any success.

"No," he replied, "I haven't seen a live deer since Tuesday." Suddenly, a doe jumped into our pig lot, and following her was a nice buck. The buck stopped hardly more than 150 feet away and looked at us. In the growing dusk I thought I detected a grin on the buck's face. Levi quickly checked his watch, which said 5:10. The season closed at five. With a wave of his tail the buck jumped across the fence, passed the pond, and the last we saw of him he was headed down the valley. Safe for another year. "Where was he all week?" Levi ruefully asked.

Maybe it is because of episodes such as this one that few words get our attention as do, "There's a deer!"

The Mysteries
of Migration

I stopped my work and listened. What at first sounded like the far-off baying of the neighbor's beagle hound turned out to be the high-pitched, almost haunting call of tundra swans. I scanned the sky and soon saw a perfect V of well over a hundred of the majestic white birds.

That mid-November day skein after skein of the swans passed high overhead, riding the currents of a strong northwest wind. After leaving their Arctic nesting grounds, they flew south to North Dakota and then turned southeast en route to their wintering grounds along Chesapeake Bay.

The mysteries of migration have aroused the human imagination for centuries. In the book of Job (39:26) we read: "Doth the hawk fly by thy wisdom and stretch her wings toward the south?" And Jeremiah (8:7) reads: "Yea, the stork in the heaven knoweth her appointed times; and the turtle and the crane and the swallow observe the time of the coming."

Aristotle was one of the first to discuss the subject of migration. He is also credited with originating the idea that birds hibernate. This hibernation theory existed for over two thousand years. Dr. Elliot Coues (1848–99), an eminent ornithologist, in 1878 listed the titles of no less than 182 papers dealing with the hibernation of swallows! The common belief was that the swallows spent their winters in the mud of marshes. It was even recorded that fishermen in northern waters sometimes caught mixed catches of fish and hibernating swallows. In the early 1700s, an even more remarkable theory suggested that birds flew to the moon and spent the winter there.

It wasn't until the advent of bird banding that these mysteries began to be unraveled. A Canadian, Jack Miner, was one of the first to use this method to study the migration patterns of ducks and geese. He not only printed his name and address on the bands but added, on the reverse side, a verse of Scripture. Miner used the birds as winged missionaries.

Since 1920, bird banding in the United States has been under the direction of the U.S. Fish and Wildlife Service. Even though band returns on nonhunted species are less than one percent, a lot has been learned about migration habits. Because waterfowl are hunted, the band returns on them are, of course, much higher. For example, on mallards the average number of bands returned the first year is around 12 percent.

The champ for long-distance travel is the arctic tern. Terns nest in the Arctic as far north as land extends in North America. After the young are grown, they leave the nesting grounds to show up, a few months later, in Antarctica, eleven thousand miles away.

Even though the arctic tern travels the farthest distance, what about some of the birds more familiar to us? Few farmers fail to thrill to the bubbling song of the spring's first bobolink. These beautiful birds of the open spaces return after spending the winter in Argentina. They nest in the hayfields and meadows, and by threshing time are already preparing to set wing for South America.

Another common spring bird that is a true transient is the water pipit. While we are working ground in April for oats, these tail-wagging sparrow-sized birds like to feed on insects stirred up by the plow and harrow. They nest in the Canadian tundra, and by the time we're sowing wheat, some pipits have already returned and again feed on insects in the same field.

The same birds? I have no way of knowing. But some experts think that migrating birds en route to and from their nesting areas may perch on the same tree visited before, drink at the same stream, and forage in the same patch of woods or field. So the water pipits in our field in September could well be the same birds that kept me company in April. The purple martins and barn swallows that many of us welcome back in late March and April winter in South America, also a considerable journey.

The spring migration is usually fairly rapid, especially for the birds that nest in the far north, whereas the fall flights are usually more leisurely. Some fall flights are fast though, as is evidenced by a young male blue-winged teal that was banded along the Athabasca River in northern Alberta and traveled thirty-eight hundred miles to Maracaibo, Venezuela, in exactly one month, for an average of 125 miles a day.

Many birds migrate during the night, and I was a witness to this several years ago. It was a warm October night with a full moon. Before going to bed, I stepped outside the house to breathe the fresh evening air, fragrant with the aroma of drying corn. The instant I looked at the moon, a V of ducks flew across its face. Though it lasted only a fraction of a second, it was a sight I'll not soon forget.

Some birds also migrate at tremendous altitudes. Climbers on Mt. Everest in 1952 found remains of a pintail and a bar-tailed godwit at 16,400 feet. Bar-headed geese have been observed flying over the highest Himalayan peaks, which would be over 29,000 feet. At 20,000 feet a man has a hard time walking, and running would be virtually impossible, but a mallard was struck by a commercial airliner at 21,000 feet over the Nevada desert. But such high flights are probably not the rule for birds; records show that two-thirds of all bird-aircraft collisions occur below 2,000 feet, and very few above 6,000 feet.

Not all birds migrate to warm climates. As I write this, our bird feeder is frequented by many visitors from Canada such as the dark-eyed junco, tree sparrows, and black-capped chickadees. This is as far south as they'll likely go so long as enough food is available. We've been hoping for some colorful evening grosbeaks, but thus far haven't had any.

During the winter of 1977–78 close to six hundred snow buntings along with some Lapland longspurs fed on cow feed (ground corn and oats) that we scattered daily in the field by the barn. These birds usually winter in the northern United States and southern Canada, but because of the extreme cold of that winter were forced farther south to find food. There are also quite a few nonmigrants at our feeder, like the brilliant cardinal which may live and die within a mile of where it was born.

It is easy for scientists and for us to understand how some birds learn to migrate—the Canada geese, for instance, migrate in family groups and flocks. All a young goose has to do is follow the leader. It is, however, more difficult to apply this imprinting to the lesser golden-plovers. The adult plovers leave their Arctic nesting grounds by early August and fly southeast to the coasts of Labrador and Nova Scotia, where they linger and lay on fat before beginning the long journey across the Atlantic to South America. Three to six weeks later their young, who were left behind in the Arctic, follow along the same route to join their parents on the Argentine Pampas. How do the young plovers know their way? "Doth the hawk fly by thy wisdom?" the voice out of the whirlwind asks Job. The implied answer is that the hawk flies by the wisdom given it by God. So do the young plovers.

Farewell to the Giants

Finishing our morning chores earlier than usual, we hurried down the pasture field through the dew-covered grass. The only sounds punctuating the stillness were a neighbor calling his cows and then the banging of milk cans being opened. After crossing the creek and several fences and fields, we reached the woods. Even in the dark the place was familiar to me. Our destination was a large red oak which we soon came to. Feeling our way to its north side, we settled down on the soft moss to await the dawn.

To the north of us we heard the pleasant gurgle of a little stream as it made its way over miniature falls and across ripples. A ghostly silent form sailed overhead, and a few minutes later, from the next wooded hill, came the hoots of a great horned owl. Gradually the sky lightened and the stars faded away. At the woods' edge a song sparrow gave his half-hearted song, which was soon followed by the whistled call of a titmouse and from high in the oak the "yank! yank!" of a nuthatch.

As the first rays of sunlight splashed across the tops of the trees, the woods came alive with daytime creatures. From a knothole near the top of a tall white oak, which to us looked closer to the size suitable for sheltering a chickadee, popped a fox squirrel. After a leisurely morning stretch and a few flicks of his bushy tail, the squirrel suddenly became ambitious and raced through the treetops to reach a beech tree. Soon the sound of beechnuts dropping through the leaves reached our ears. It seemed that all roads led to the beech, as a red-headed woodpecker, three bluejays, and several more squirrels headed that way.

Then from the road to the east came the ringing of steel wagon wheels on gravel. The sound died out as the team and wagon turned into a field. It was replaced by a man's voice rising in song, and since this was the week off from school for corn husking, children's voices were soon blending in harmony. Though the distance was great, the words carried clearly across the browning fields and through the golden trees. We were roused from our reverie when the first ears of corn hit the bangboards—a reminder that our corn, too, was waiting.

My son and I came to this woods for a special purpose. I wanted him to see what this country was like when the first settlers arrived from across the Appalachians. And I had come to bid farewell to a place I had visited many times over the years. In my early years, I often accompanied my father here and later I would come by myself. I'm not sure whether it was by a quirk of topography or the desire of the family that settled the land that this remnant of virgin woods was preserved in the southwest corner of the farm, bordered on the north by a stream and marsh and along the east side by a deep ravine. It was, at any rate, virtually impossible to log with horses. Whatever the reason, the magnificent trees were spared the axe for 150 years after the farm was deeded.

For over a hundred years the land was farmed by the descendants of the original settlers. Following the depression years, the industry of northern cities beckoned, and the sons left to work in factories, manufacturing the machinery that would replace them on the farm. After their father's death, the farm was rented to tenant farmers. I am too young to remember the first renters, but the ones I do remember were all good farmers.

Every family eventually left to buy its own farm. As the years passed, the buildings began to deteriorate because very little money was forthcoming from the owners for repairs. Finally it became difficult to find renters because the house was in such disrepair.

Then just a few days before our visit to the woods a neighbor told me, "The farm has been sold to a nephew of the owners." I felt a stab of concern, and not without reason, because he added, "And he has already sold the timber." Since most people are not too reverent about trees, and modern technology recognizes few natural barriers, I knew the woods were doomed.

Arising from our cushiony bed of moss, we walked through the woods to look and admire for the last time. We paused beneath red and white oaks and poplars towering sixty feet to their first limbs. Their branches, joining high overhead, gave the impression of a green-and-gold cathedral ceiling supported by massive wooden columns. In autumns past, like my older brothers before me, I would often take a morning off on the pretense of hunting for squirrels to come here and revel in this grandeur—an experience both humbling and exhilarating.

Standing on the edge of a shaded bank carpeted with Christmas ferns was an ancient beech tree. Carved on it were the initials and date, "JK 1944," and slightly to the side of this was a carving that brought back memories of my own school-day adventures: "IW & DK CAUGHT 6 SKUNKS. FEB. 1958," along with an arrow pointing to several woodchuck burrows at the base of the beech.

Coming to the edge of the woods, we followed the stream to where it flowed past the barnyard. I wanted to see the barn. Some siding and sections of metal from the roof were missing, but the timbers were still pretty straight and solid. The floor was worn from the pounding hoofs of teams as loads of hay were hauled into the barn. This barn, which at one time was filled to the rafters with the bounty of the fields, held the hopes and dreams of the farmer and echoed with the shouts and laughter of his children, was silent now.

It was here on this farm that my dad, for the first time, sent me instead of my brother as a hand to fill the silo. From that year on I was part of the silo-filling crew. Working here among the "hills and hollers" was always enjoyable, and I was sorry when I realized the silo was filled for the last time. That year the silo was full by noon, and those of us that worked in the field stood around waiting while the last load was put through the filler before heading to the house for dinner. We were suddenly startled when someone hollered, "The silo! It's falling!" Sure enough, ever so slowly, the gap between the barn and wooden silo was widening. Dan, the farmer, and a neighbor boy, Little Enos, were on top of the silage. With strong arms Dan tossed Little Enos to the roof of the barn and quickly climbed down the chute. Someone grabbed a hayrope, looped it around one of the top hoops, and we tied it to a beam on the inside of the barn, thus stopping the silo's descent. Many of us were afraid that, should the silo decide to continue its journey, it would take the old barn right down with it.

When my son and I walked around the end of the barn, I noticed that the silo was gone. Crossing two fields, we came to the sugar camp. This was about a two-acre grove of sugar maples along with a few oak and hickory trees. In the center, on a slight rise, was the sugar shanty. Since this was part of the pasture, it was almost parklike beneath the grand old sugar trees. At the east edge of the grove, on top of a shaded knoll, the ground covered with myrtle, was the cemetery where the pioneer family was buried.

After climbing up the embankment, we rested in the cool shade of the cemetery trees. Partly to reassure myself, I said to my son, "At least these trees will be spared. Surely they won't cut trees that were nourished on the pioneer family." One tree, a linden, grew out of two-year-old Jonathan's grave. Next to him was his one-year-old sister, Angeline. I could almost see the grieving family here on the knoll. The singing of the vireos and the scarlet tanager likely went unnoticed.

From the cemetery it was only a short distance to our farm. Before going over the hill we turned and paused for one last look at the beauty of the unspoiled woods.

Later on that fall, the quietness of the countryside was shattered one morning by the snarl of chain saws, and soon afterward by the whine of the power log skidders. At times I would become aware of a saw being shut off and then a thunderous crash. Soon smoke-belching diesel trucks began rumbling past our place laden with the mammoth logs. The very finest of these trees that had survived storm and heat for over a quarter of a millennium, furnished food and shelter to bird and beast, and thrilled the hearts of everyone who saw them, would be exported to Europe.

As is so often the case, the landowner was misled by a shrewd timber buyer. The agreement was that any tree fourteen inches and over in diameter could be taken. However, this was at an undetermined height. Naturally, almost any tree ten inches across will flare to fourteen inches at ground level. No doubt, it can be argued that many of the older trees were "ripe to harvest." But there is no justifiable excuse, I believe, for cutting down a healthy ten-inch white oak. Wouldn't it have been better to use the trees to rebuild the barn and house, and to make furniture, so that some young family could again care for and prosper on the farmstead? The land is still being well farmed by neighbors. One of them told me recently, "The land produces good crops. But now nobody could afford to buy it for there is no timber left for new buildings."

From a distance and while filling a silo at the neighboring farm, I could see a few gnarled fingers of trees pointing skyward. These were trees that didn't "measure up." For some reason I had no desire to return. And yet I knew that some day I had to go back and see the devastation for myself.

In the fourth autumn I went back, not with the confidence of someone on familiar ground, but more like a stranger in an alien land. As I walked across the farm, I was astounded at the change that had taken place. The large oaks that had shaded the pasture, the maples and wild cherries along the fencerows and roadsides, the sycamores by the creek, even the shade trees around the farm buildings—all were gone. When I reached the virgin part of the woods, I found treetops scattered everywhere, almost hidden by brambles, pokeberries, and new tree seedlings. I was saddened by the realization that something old and beautiful was lost. The primeval forest, once home to the squirrel, raccoon, and pileated, had become an impenetrable jungle, a haven for the cottontail, gray fox, and catbird. I tried walking down the stream, and after crawling over and beneath the branches that crisscrossed the creek, I finally reached the giant beech. It was lying on its carvings—hollow, of no economic value and so left to rot.

The sugar camp had fared no better. What used to be a pleasant shaded place was now open pasture. At least here the treetops had been cut up for firewood. All that remained were the stumps—I counted sixty-four—of the grand old maple trees. Upon checking the stumps, I noticed many were hollow. Hardly grade lumber, more likely pallet wood. To me it doesn't seem fair for this beautiful grove of trees that provided the pleasures of sugaring in March, refreshing shade for the cattle in summer, and brilliant colors in October, to have been cut and nailed into pallets to be used one time and then burned in the firepit of some distant industrial park.

The first thing I noticed as I climbed the knoll to the cemetery was the lack of shade. The shade-loving myrtle was being choked out by briars and weeds and, as I reached the top, my first thought was that nothing is sacred anymore. Jonathan's linden was gone to share the fate of the sugar maples, and so were the large white oaks on either side of it. The gravemarkers were lying helter-skelter and some were broken. Whether crushed by the falling trees or the skidder, I don't know. I knelt down and carefully turned over a marker. As I gently cleaned the dirt off its face and fitted the pieces together, the motif appeared and then the name: ANGELINE.

Beyond the Seasons

The American Chestnut

Along the edge of our woods, at what long ago used to be a corner of a field, lies the gray skeleton of a giant chestnut tree. It has been there for as long as I can remember, tenaciously resisting decay. The magnificent tree was likely spared the axe when the pioneer Eshelman family settled the land in 1825 because of the delicious and abundant nuts it provided each autumn. And no doubt it provided pleasant shade beneath its spreading branches for the men and their teams during harvest time. It succumbed to the deadly chestnut blight, probably during the 1920s.

When I happen to come across these relics of times past, I can't help but feel somewhat cheated—I have never tasted an American chestnut. The older people of the community tell me that the imported Chinese chestnuts are, at best, only a fair substitute for the smaller but sweeter native chestnut.

When the first settlers arrived, fully 25 percent and in some places 40 percent of the forests were chestnuts. They were fast-growing trees, adding up to an inch in diameter annually, reaching four feet and sometimes more across the stump. For instance, in the Smoky Mountain National Park a fallen, dead chestnut measured nine feet six inches in diameter; and at sixty-five feet from the ground, it still measured four feet eight inches across.

The rot-resistant wood was widely used for rail fences. We

have several sections of rail fence in our yard that were split in the early years of this century. Besides being used for fences, the knot-free wood was used for barn siding, tool handles, wagon tongues, church benches, and furniture.

Not only were the nuts relished by humans, but the deer, squirrels, raccoons, bears, and turkeys fattened on them each fall.

Nobody could have believed, in the late eighteenth century, that anything could happen to these stately and useful trees.

Then came the blight.

The chestnut blight was first observed in New York City in 1904. It is believed to have been introduced by a contaminated Chinese chestnut acquired by the New York Zoological Park. From New York the dreaded killer marched steadily west and south. Even though the chestnut trees were vigorous and healthy, they were genetically defenseless against the invader.

The blight is a fungus whose spores, spread by wind, animals, and birds, enter the inner bark through openings in the outer bark. Since chestnut trees are exceptionally fast growing, cracks in the bark are common. The fungus then penetrates the sapwood and grows by releasing enzymes that break down the chestnut cells. At these points of entry cankers are formed, which look like rough, corky swellings of the bark and usually appear on the main trunk. Eventually these cankers encircle the tree and, just as surely as if it had been girdled by an axe, they kill it.

The blight never killed the roots, so many of the old chestnut stumps kept sending up sprouts. Some of these produced nuts before they, too, succumbed to the parasitic fungus. A few years ago I saw on a ridge in the southwestern part of our county dozens of chestnut stumps that had sprouts twenty to thirty feet high and eight to ten inches in diameter—but all were dead. Grim reminders of man's meddling.

In less than fifty years after its discovery in New York, the blight had killed virtually all the large chestnuts from New England through the Appalachians to the western edge of its range. To underscore the enormity of this loss, a U.S. Forest Service scientist estimated that all the timber lost to the blight would be valued at four hundred billion dollars on today's market.

Many of the dead trees were cut down and sawn into lumber. My uncle told how he helped a farmer harvest his dead chestnut timber during 1931 and '32. They had their own sawmill and, during periods when the farmwork was slack, they sawed over seventy-five thousand board feet which was then sold at very depressed prices. He said they should have waited several years because by then wormy chestnut was in great demand as a finishing wood.

There are, however, a few isolated groves of mature, nut-producing trees in Michigan and Wisconsin that have been untouched by the blight. Scientists think that these were started by settlers bringing along nuts and seedlings from the East 150 years ago. All told, there are several thousand small trees and around five hundred mature ones in these areas.

Is there any hope for the American chestnut? Some horticultural and forest scientists think there is. Most of the past efforts at conservation have been attempts to breed blight-resistant trees, and this hasn't been too successful. Yet any chestnut surviving today in blight areas must have a certain degree of blight resistance. The tragedy is that most of these trees do not produce nuts. I know of one such tree—it blooms and produces burrs but no nuts. Apparently it is not self-pollinating. The efforts to produce hybrid blight-resistant trees by crossing Chinese and American chestnuts haven't worked either.

At the present time the method that shows the most promise involves using a weaker strain of fungus that, for reasons not yet totally understood, weakens the deadly virulent strain of fungus. Cankers on diseased chestnuts that have been inoculated with this strain (called hypovirulent) have either stopped growing or healed completely in the majority of the tests.

The problem now is to get this "friendly" fungus to spread by itself as it has in Europe. Thus far, it has not flourished as scientists had hoped, though some Michigan chestnuts with cankers caused by blight have been surviving and healing. The strain of blight turned out to be the first known hypovirulent strain to develop in America. And so the foresters and plant pathologists are optimistic. Who knows, maybe in the future we can again enjoy sitting, as Longfellow wrote, "Under the spreading chestnut tree . . ."

Aliens

A black, stocky bird with a smattering of yellowish spots and a bright yellow bill lit on the martin house. After a few attempts at whistled song along with a halfhearted flapping of wings, it was joined by its similar-looking mate. The bold bird then proceeded in a nervous, hurried manner to inspect the nesting compartments, while the martins milled around the house, voicing their protests. Measures had to be taken to counter the bird's brazen behavior. The intruder was, naturally, a European starling.

The starling, along with the house sparrow, common pigeon, Norway rat, and, in the streams and lakes, the German carp, would rank high on the list of wildlife pests. All are relative newcomers to North America. And every one of them except the rat was deliberately brought to America in the misguided belief that it would enhance the lives of the human population.

The Norway rats probably came over as stowaways on the many sailing vessels plying the Atlantic. During the nights they marched down the gangplanks and made themselves at home in the bustling port cities. From the seaports the rodents spread across the country.

In 1850, the Brooklyn Institute in New York appointed a committee to introduce the house sparrow (or English sparrow) to the United States. That year, eight pairs were brought from England to the Institute where they were cared for in cages during the winter months and then released the following spring. To the chagrin of the committee the sparrows didn't thrive. Not given to defeat, they tried again the next year. A large number of sparrows were shipped to America aboard the steamship *Europa* and let loose in Brooklyn's Greenwood Cemetery. This time the spunky birds survived and began multiplying. In 1860, a dozen imported sparrows were lovingly released in Madison Square, and four years after that more were released in Central Park.

One of the reasons for bringing the sparrows to the United States was that they had the reputation of being prolific breeders and voracious eaters of insects, and it was hoped they would end a plague of cankerworms that were eating the leaves of shade trees. The sparrows did live up to their reputation as breeders, and they did destroy some insects, mainly as food for nestlings. The adults, however, preferred the undigested grain in horse droppings. And with all the horses in the cities in the mid-eighteen hundreds, America was the sparrows' promised land.

Not to be outdone by New York, almost every city east of the Mississippi River soon wanted house sparrows. The sparrow became a status symbol; to have the birds building their messy nests in the cornices of the courthouse was a sign of progress.

Cleveland, Ohio, bought their sparrows in 1869. In the same year, the city government of Philadelphia, Pennsylvania, decided to go about the sparrow business in a big way. It imported a thousand birds and turned them loose. In 1876, Dubuque, Iowa, purchased twenty pairs, as did many other cities and towns. By 1886 the now slightly less-loved birds were in every state east of the Mississippi and in several states west of it.

Gradually, following a reluctant awakening, the tide of public opinion turned against the house sparrow and its bad habits. But it was too late; the pests were firmly established. Nothing that the cities and counties tried—bounties, nest de-

struction, and trapping—had any lasting effect on what the
eminent ornithologist, Dr. Elliot Coues, called "the sturdy little foreign vulgarians." The sparrows not only did not eat the
insects they were supposed to eat, but they chased away, and
eventually displaced, the native birds that normally did eat
these insects. The eastern bluebird probably suffered more
than any other single species from the boisterous sparrow's invasion. In the early nineteen hundreds, Jack Miner, the famous Canadian naturalist, wrote, "The chief cause of the decrease of the bluebird is English sparrows. One of man's great
mistakes was when he introduced this little, domineering Bol-
shevik into America."

Possibly the greatest tragedy of the house sparrow fiasco
was that so few people seemed to have learned from the mis-
take. By 1890 New York City was at it again. This time, a drug
manufacturer, Eugene Scheifflin, whose hobbies were the
study of birds and of Shakespeare, came up with the notion to
import to America all the bird species that Shakespeare mentioned in his writings. Unfortunately, the starling was mentioned, and Scheifflin duly imported and released sixty starlings in Central Park. Their first nests were built under the
eaves of the American Museum of Natural History, and young
were successfully fledged.

From Central Park the aggressive birds, who do nothing in
moderation, spread across North America. In 1952, one was
sighted near Juneau, Alaska. The starling's conquest of the
continent, excluding Greenland and the Arctic regions, was
complete.

Like the house sparrow, the starling is by preference a cavity
nester. So again the native birds that suffered were the cavity
nesters: the bluebirds, purple martins, tree swallows, and especially the woodpeckers.

The common pigeon, called rock dove in the bird books, is
also an immigrant. This close companion of city-dwellers, be-

loved by poets and philosophers, was first introduced to the shores of the New World by the French at Port Royal, Nova Scotia, in 1606. Not nearly the pest that the house sparrow and starling are, the pigeon nevertheless has become a nuisance in many cities where flocks of thousands thrive.

Public health officials especially are concerned because the pigeon is a carrier of chlamydiosis, a disease occasionally fatal to birds and animals. Of all known carriers of the disease, the pigeon is the most common. Because of the threat of disease, some cities have an annual pigeon shoot to reduce the number of birds hanging around the courthouse belfry.

Here in the country the pigeons are never the pests they are in the cities. The male's cooing as he struts across the barn beams wooing his mate is beautiful when compared to the annoying chatter of a pair of house sparrows busily stuffing the hay carrier with grass and straw for their nest. Another reason that pigeons around here don't reach nuisance numbers is that they have market value. Hardly a summer passes when we aren't awakened by farm boys banging on the door at midnight, asking permission to catch pigeons.

A classic example of ecological ignorance is the importation and widespread stocking of the carp. For this we thank Rudolph Hessel, a fish culturist for the United States government, who firmly believed that the carp was the finest fish in the world. In the fall of 1876, he was sent to Europe to bring back a shipment of these fish. The trip was a failure, for on the way home the ship encountered rough seas in the North Atlantic and, on arrival in Boston, every one of the wonderful carp was dead.

Hessel did not give up, however. The following spring he again traveled to Germany, carefully selected 345 more carp, and on May 26, 1877, he landed at New York with every fish alive and vigorous. After stocking some ponds in Boston with his prize fish, Hessel journeyed to Washington to receive the applause of a grateful Congress. He was convinced that the carp would quickly outclass our native fish.

Because of all the publicity surrounding the new wonder fish, people were practically lining up to get breeding stock. Congressmen haggled to see that their own districts got their fair share. By 1879 over twelve thousand carp were released in twenty-five states and territories and, in 1883, two hundred sixty thousand of the fish were distributed among 298 congressional districts. Only three districts were left without carp. Tragically, many of the carp were released into these districts' finest and most pristine waters.

After a few years, reports of the carp's fine progress began arriving in Washington. In 1884 it was reported to the U.S. Fish Commissioner that a three-and-a-half-pound carp from the James River in Virginia appeared at a fish market. Closer to my home, in the May 15, 1890, issue of *The Sugarcreek Budget* was this report: "Several very fine large carp have been caught in Sugarcreek this spring. On last Sat. Mr. Levi Hostetler succeeded in landing one which measured 16 in. in length and weighed 2¾ lbs. and on the same day Mr. John Deetz captured one that weighed 3 lbs. Two years ago several thousand young carp were placed in the creek by owners of ponds and the results speak well for the deed."

Soon the novelty of the new immigrant began to wear off, and to the surprise of Rudolph Hessel and the politicians the praises of its excellence came to an abrupt end.

In waters where the carp increased, fishing for the native fish became less and less productive. The carp now became the villain and was accused of eating fish, ruining spawning beds, and rooting up wild rice and celery. Furthermore, it lost its status as a game fish, for many anglers considered the carp unfit to eat. By 1900, Lake Erie commercial fishermen were appealing to the government for help to eradicate the "Great Lakes salmon," as the carp was sometimes called in eastern markets.

But again, as with the sparrows and starlings, it was too late to undo the damage done. The carp, or "sewer bass" as some fishermen disdainfully call it, was here to stay.

Not only did the native fish pay a price for this ecological boondoggle but the waterfowl suffered as well. Before the arrival of the carp, Lake Koshkonong in Wisconsin was visited by thousands of migrating canvasbacks every fall. What was attractive to these handsome ducks was the wild celery which abounded in the lake and was their favorite food. In 1880, the lake was stocked with carp. The fish rooted out the wild celery; as it disappeared from Koshkonong, so did the canvasbacks. The same thing happened to the wild celery in the fertile, shallow waters of western Lake Erie. This part of the Great Lakes once offered some of the finest canvasback hunting in the country. A terrible price—carp for canvasbacks.

There have been, on the other hand, a few cases of alien bird stockings that were successful, notably the ring-necked pheasant and the chukar. Both of these Asian birds seem to occupy a niche in America's natural world not previously occupied by any native species.

Hundreds of other attempted introductions fortunately failed, as I wish the starlings had. And I can't help wondering if we'd have an easier time keeping purple martins nesting around the house had Shakespeare not penned the line in *Henry IV*, "Nay, I'll have a starling shall be taught to speak nothing but 'Mortimer.'"

XZ 89

One day last December, a flock of thirty geese came winging in to our pond. We could tell that these Canadians were strangers because six of them sported colorful neck bands. Three of the collars were blue and three were orange. On each collar were four large numbers and letters. With our twenty-power telescope we could make out the code on four of them, two blue and two orange, which I then dutifully reported to the Department of Natural Resources. The geese stayed in the area for about a week and then continued southward.

When winter turned into spring and I had almost forgotten about the bands I had reported, the mailman brought us a letter from the U.S. Fish and Wildlife Service. The letter said that the two blue-collared geese were banded at Henderson, Kentucky, only a few weeks before they stopped at our pond. Contrary to the usual fall migration pattern, these geese had traveled north several hundred miles before heading back south. The letter gave no information on the orange bands.

In July, however, an envelope arrived, postmarked Moosonee, from the Ontario Ministry of Natural Resources. Since I knew that Moosonee was somewhere near Hudson's or James Bay, I eagerly ripped open the envelope. The letter, from the ministry's district manager, said that the goose, an adult male, with the code XZ 89 on its neck-collar had been banded on July 18, 1986, forty-eight miles northeast of Attawapiskat, Ontario. The other one, an adult female, was banded two days later, sixty-four miles northeast of the same village.

The letter continued: "Approximately 7000 Canada geese are banded annually by the Ontario Ministry of Natural Resources in cooperation with the Mississippi Waterfowl Flyway Council. About half of this total is banded on Akimiski Island and half along the Hudson and James Bay coast of Ontario. All of the geese are banded on the leg with a metal band with a unique number code. Adults are additionally neck-collared with orange plastic collars, each bird having a unique 4 character code—its "name" which identifies it by sight."

On the map, the village of Attawapiskat is near the mouth of the river bearing the same name, which is about halfway up the western coast of James Bay. In the bay, just outside the mouth of the river, is Akimiski Island where the geese were banded.

Neck-collaring has obvious advantages. The geese don't have to be shot or recaptured in order to read the bands. Because of this method, we now know that the Canadian honker XZ 89, after being banded on Akimiski Island, flew almost due south to rest and feed here in December. Maybe our farm now shows as a tiny colored pin on a migration wall map somewhere marking where XZ 89 was "sited." Interesting. But is this information really necessary? Is it necessary enough to justify requiring XZ 89 and the other neck-banded geese to wear those annoying plastic collars for the rest of their lives?

It seems that some of our wildlife is being literally researched to death. The black-footed ferret is a good example. These small weasel-like animals live in prairie dog towns. They were considered to be on the edge of extinction when a colony was discovered in September 1981 on a private ranch in Wyoming. Actually, the credit of rediscovery belongs to a ranch dog named Shep. Shep "collected" one, as biologists like to say, several inches from his food dish. The owners couldn't identify Shep's victim, so they called the Fish and Wildlife Service. The animal was quickly identified as a black-footed ferret. Now the search began for a live ferret, and the colony was subsequently found about five miles from where the one was killed.

The owners of the land where the ferrets were located didn't believe in poisoning prairie dogs, so their ranch still had thousands of the burrowing rodents. Naturally, what was good for prairie dogs was good for black-footed ferrets.

A mark and recapture program was started to monitor the ferrets. In September 1984 the survey indicated a thriving population of 128. As researchers swarmed over the area by day and wildlife photographers by night, a nightmare began to unfold. By August of the following year, the population estimate had dropped to sixty and by October to thirty-one. The ferrets were dying. Likewise, the prairie dogs, who were also dying in astounding numbers, were diagnosed as having sylvatic plague. This bacterial disease is spread by fleas. In humans it is called bubonic plague or Black Death.

To slow the plague, it was decided to kill the fleas. The state bought thirteen thousand pounds of Sevin and dusted around and into one hundred thousand prairie dogs' burrows. Nothing was known about the insecticide's effect on ferrets. It was known, however, to stop dogs from scratching. Despite the effort to preserve them, the ferrets kept on dying.

The Wyoming Game and Fish Department then live-trapped six ferrets with the intention of starting a captive breeding program. Soon one of the captured ferrets died of distemper. It must have been infected before it was trapped. This viral disease is usually associated with dogs, but it can infect and kill many other animals, including ferrets. It is thought that the deadly disease could very possibly have been carried to the ferret colony on the clothing of a biologist or photographer from an infected pet at home.

By January 1986, all six captive ferrets were dead. Another six trapped the previous fall were still alive, so the decision was made to trap the dozen or so remaining in the wild. All were caught except one wily ferret that evaded the biologists through the summer and fall until it was dug out of a burrow in February 1987. So, like the last free-flying California condor, the last-known black-footed ferret is now confined to a cage.

If that one footloose ferret hadn't ventured so close to Shep's dinner dish, it may well be that the colony at Meeteetse, Wyoming, would still be thriving. The adage, "If it's not broken, don't fix it," holds true in nature too.

In a recent essay about misguided wildlife research, outdoor writer Gene Hill wrote, "I have nothing against scientific observation, census, or just plain curiosity. I am as interested as the next ignoramus about the curious life cycle of the migrating butterfly or the whereabouts of the black-footed ferrets, but I think there are some technological gadgets that we could resist in the name of decency, even if life is a little more incomplete without them."

When I think of the stately gander, XZ 89, shaking his head and then with his bill attempting to remove the ugly plastic neck-collar, I can't help agreeing with Gene Hill.

Extinct and
Endangered Birds

"In the autumn of 1813, I left my house at Henderson, on the banks of the Ohio, on my way to Louisville. In passing over the Barrens a few miles beyond Hardensburgh, I observed the pigeons flying from northeast to southwest, in greater numbers than I thought I had ever seen them before, and feeling an inclination to count the flocks that might pass within the reach of my eye in one hour, I dismounted, seated myself on an eminence, and began to mark with my pencil, making a dot for every flock that passed. In a short time finding the task which I had undertaken impracticable, as the birds poured in countless multitudes, I rose, and counting the dots then put down, found that 163 had been made in twenty-one minutes. The air was literally filled with pigeons; the light of noonday was obscured as by an eclipse.

"Before sunset I reached Louisville, distant from Hardensburgh fifty-three miles. The pigeons were still passing in undiminished numbers, and continued to do so for three days in succession.

"It may not, perhaps, be out of place to attempt an estimate of the number of pigeons contained in one of those mighty flocks, and of the quantity of food daily consumed by its members. The inquiry will tend to show the astonishing bounty of the great Author of Nature in providing the wants of his creatures. Let us take a column of one mile in breadth, which is below the average size, and suppose it flies over us without interruption for three hours, at the rate mentioned above of one mile in the minute. This will give us a parallelogram of 180 miles by 1, covering 180 square miles. Allowing two pigeons to the square yard, we have one billion, one hundred and fifteen millions, one hundred thirty-six thousand pigeons in one flock. As every pigeon daily consumes fully half a pint of food, the quantity necessary for supplying this vast multitude must be eight millions, seven hundred and twelve thousand bushel per day.

"On such occasions, when the woods are filled with these pigeons, they are killed in immense numbers. Persons unacquainted with these birds might naturally conclude that such dreadful havoc would soon put an end to the species. But I have satisfied myself, by long observation, that nothing but the gradual diminution of our forests can accomplish their decrease, as they not infrequently quadruple their numbers yearly, and at least double it."

When John James Audubon wrote these words in his *Ornithological Biography* he didn't realize that a century later, on September 1, 1914, the last survivor of these vast hordes of passenger pigeons would die in the Cincinnati Zoo.

Some authorities estimated that there were probably five billion pigeons in the three states of Kentucky, Ohio, and Indiana alone. In May 1866 a northward flight was reported in Ontario, Canada, that was at least three hundred miles long, a mile wide, and continued for fourteen hours; the flock contained an estimated three billion, seven hundred seventeen million birds.

Because of the pigeons' seemingly limitless numbers, the birds were slaughtered relentlessly. From one nesting colony in Michigan alone, twenty-five thousand pigeons were killed daily for the market for twenty-eight days by professional netters. Even though they were killed by the millions and sold for one or two cents apiece, the thought that the passenger pigeon was doomed to extinction never occurred to the market hunters. In the mid-1800s a select committee of the Ohio State Senate reported, "The passenger pigeon needs no protection." How wrong they were.

In less than two hundred years North Americans have wiped out at least five species of the continent's birds, a record unmatched on any comparable land mass in the world. By contrast, Europe has not lost a single species in its recorded history.

The first bird to go was the great auk. These big, flightless birds inhabited rocky islands in the North Atlantic. Because these auks were helpless on land, enormous numbers were killed in their nesting colonies by sailors for food and by fishermen for bait. The last remnants of these once numerous birds were taken by commercial hunters who clubbed them to death and stripped off their feathers for use in pillows and mattresses. The last great auk died on June 3, 1844, seven years before Audubon's death.

By then, the Labrador duck, the next bird to disappear, was already extremely rare. This black-and-white sea duck was evidently never very abundant anywhere in its range, although from 1840 to 1860 fair numbers appeared in New York markets. One New Yorker wrote, "It was not unusual to see them in Fulton Market. At one time I remember seeing six fine males, which hung in the market until spoiled for the want of a purchaser; they were not considered desirable for the table." The last-known Labrador duck was shot by a boy on December 12, 1878, on Long Island, New York, and was eaten by the boy's family. Only the head and neck were preserved, but these too were eventually lost. All that now remains of this beautiful sea duck are forty-four stuffed specimens in museums scattered throughout the world.

The next bird to become extinct was the passenger pigeon,

and, only four years after the pigeon's demise, the last surviving Carolina parakeet died, also at the Cincinnati Zoo. This colorful bird was the only member of the parrot family native to the United States. It ranged from the Southeast, west to Texas, Kansas, and Nebraska. This gregarious bird was killed by admirers and enemies alike. In the late 1800s it became fashionable to adorn ladies' hats with feathers, plumes, and even entire birds. The parakeets were in great demand by the millinery trade because of their brilliant green and yellow plumage, and so were pursued without mercy by market hunters. At the same time, since they were seed and fruit eaters and had existed on cypress nuts, thistles, and cockleburs, they quickly adapted to feeding on fruits in planted orchards. As they destroyed unripened apples, peaches, and oranges, the birds were shot by outraged farmers. The survivors had the unfortunate habit of circling back over the dead and wounded, becoming themselves easy targets for the gunmen. Entire flocks were killed in this manner. The guns had to be turned elsewhere when the last Carolina parakeet died in September of 1918.

The fifth species to vanish was the heath hen. This eastern counterpart of the greater prairie chicken ranged from Massachusetts south along the Atlantic seaboard to Virginia. By the turn of the century, after its numbers had been reduced to less than a hundred birds by market and pothunters, the heath hen made its last stand on Martha's Vineyard. Assisted by the efforts and protection of the Massachusetts Department of Conservation, the colony increased to several thousand birds by 1916. And then disaster struck. In May a great fire swept across the island, burning the brooding birds and reducing their numbers to around 150, mostly males. Domestic poultry diseases and several hard winters further reduced the population to thirteen by 1927. The next fall, only two birds were left and, by December, only one. This lone bird, a male, was last seen on March 11, 1932.

Several other species, including the ivory-billed woodpecker, Eskimo curlew, and Bachman's warbler are on the verge of extinction. Although it is still being searched for in the old-growth river forests of the southern states, the ivory-billed woodpecker may already be extinct. Even bigger than the crow-sized pileated woodpecker, the magnificent ivory bill began to disappear as the great cypress swamps and river bottoms were cut out and drained. There have been no confirmed sightings in this country in recent years.

The Eskimo curlew was thought at one time to be extinct. But it was "rediscovered" and is now seen occasionally during migration, usually along the Texas coast and always in small numbers, a far cry from this upland shorebird's former abundance. In July 1833 Audubon had seen flocks of curlews along the Labrador coast, so large they reminded him of the vast numbers of passenger pigeons. They were also reported to visit Newfoundland by the millions.

The curlew was popular as a gamebird, and was often called "dough-bird" for the reason reported by a gunner: "It was so fat when it reached us in the fall that its breast would often burst open when it fell to the ground, and the thick layer of fat was so soft that it felt like a ball of dough." No wonder it was highly prized by the market hunters. The greatest killings were made on the westen plains during the spring migration when the curlews would congregate in huge flocks; wagonloads of the plump birds would be shot. Arthur Bent in his *Life Histories* reports, "There was no difficulty in getting quite close to the birds, perhaps within 25 or 35 yards, and when at about this distance the hunters would wait for them to arise on their feet, which was the signal for the first volley of shots. The startled birds would rise and circle about the field for a few times, affording ample opportunity for further murderous discharge of the guns, and sometimes would realight on the same field, when the attack would be repeated. One person has killed as many as thirty-seven curlews with a pump gun at one rise. Sometimes the bunch would be seen with the glass, alighting in a field two or three miles away, when the hunters would at once drive to that field with a horse and buggy as rapidly as they could and resume the fusillade and slaughter." By 1890 the Eskimo curlews were no longer seen in great numbers, and on April 17, 1915, one was killed near Norwalk, Nebraska, the last one reported shot in the United States. Only a remnant remains.

To quote Bent again, "The story of the Eskimo curlew is just one more pitiful tale of the slaughter of the innocents. It is a sad fact that the countless swarms of this fine bird and the passenger pigeon, which once swept across our land on migrations, are gone forever, sacrificed to the insatiable greed of man."

Unlike the Eskimo curlew, the Bachman's warbler was probably never an abundant bird and had a much more restricted range. Yet between 1886 and 1888 close to forty of these rare warblers were shot for the millinery trade from one area in Louisiana. So it seems that the Bachman's warbler, too, became "a victim on Fashion's altar." It is now so rare that Roger Tory Peterson, the author of *A Field Guide to the Birds*, has never seen one.

The California condor, North America's largest soaring land bird, now exists only in captivity. Driven to the brink of extinction, these birds are now being carefully raised by biologists who are hoping to insure the birds' comeback.

The whooping crane, whose wingspread is almost as wide as the condor's, is steadily coming back from a low of fifteen birds in 1937. Wintering at Aransas National Wildlife Refuge in Texas, they make the long eighteen-hundred-mile flight to

Wood Buffalo National Park in northern Alberta, where they nest and raise their young. All told, there are now close to two hundred cranes in the wild and in captivity.

Other species that are still endangered are the Kirtland's warbler, the peregrine falcon, and the snail (formerly Everglade) kite. These, however, with protection and assistance from man, seem to be holding their own. And several species that hovered on the edge of extinction at the turn of the century have made remarkable comebacks, notably the wood duck and the wild turkey. From very low populations, these have rebounded until now both number in the millions again.

But overall our record is nothing to be proud of. God gave man "dominion over the fish of the sea, and over the fowls of the air, and over the cattle and over all the earth, and over every creeping thing that creepeth upon the earth." Are we to be wise stewards, or does this give us the right to exploit, abuse, and exterminate His Creation?

Planting
for Wildlife

Last December two of our children and I participated in the annual Christmas Bird Count sponsored locally by The Wilderness Center in Wilmot, Ohio, and nationally by the National Audubon Society.

As we walked the four miles of woods and farmland allotted to us, we saw a sprinkling of the typical winter birds, but nothing unusual. This changed, however, as we approached the lower end of a small, brushy ravine. We immediately spotted a number of cardinals and a rufous-sided towhee. The birds were moving toward an adjacent woods; I went around to the opposite side so that we wouldn't miss any of the birds as they left the cover. We could hardly believe our eyes as we counted twenty-seven cardinals, nine white-throated sparrows, five tufted titmice, four chickadees, two cedar waxwings, one hermit thrush, a brown thrasher, and the towhee. Since we didn't walk through the ravine for fear of unduly disturbing the birds' haven, we no doubt missed quite a few.

What was so attractive about this ravine, which couldn't have been larger than half an acre, that all these birds congregated there? Why did the brown thrasher linger when most others of its kind had long since migrated to warmer climes? The answer was obvious. The ravine fulfilled the birds' basic need for food, water, and shelter.

The ravine was a thicket of multiflora roses, blackberry brambles, and wild grapes. These not only provided food in the form of rose hips and dried grapes but also offered protection from predators and inclement weather. The trickle of spring water that flowed through the gully provided open water throughout the winter—perfect habitat for birds.

It is possible to make improvements in wildlife habitat. Whether one lives on a farm or on a city property that has only a backyard, much can be done by planting desirable trees, shrubs, and vines. These plantings provide sanctuary for many species of wildlife and also enhance the beauty of the homestead. In addition, many of these are double-duty plants—useful both to wildlife and to us.

Since there are so many useful species of plants, I will speak of just a scattering of easily recognized natives. First, we'll consider the backyard, as this is the spot where many of us desire to attract more wildlife.

Though wildlife love it, the multiflora rose has fallen into disgrace because of its undesirable habit of spreading by seed and root, until some woods and fields, where it grows unchecked, have become impenetrable jungles. In fact, it is now illegal to plant it in some states. The Soil Conservation Service now promotes another alien, the autumn olive, as an alternative to the multiflora. It, too, tends to spread by seed, and we have found it to be a very inconsistent fruit bearer.

A much more desirable shrub for the backyard and one that is just as attractive to the birds is the native gray dogwood (*Cornus racemosa*). This shrub grows to a height of eight to twelve feet, and can be planted as a seedling, or as a rooted or unrooted cutting. Creamy white clusters of flowers are scattered over the bushes in early summer, and by the end of September the berries ripen. Close to one hundred species of birds eat these dogwood berries, and we've had yellow-rumped warblers stay into early winter in order to feast on them. One disadvantage is that the troublesome starlings, too, relish the buckshot-sized fruits.

Another shrub, the elderberry, is useful in a number of ways. The flat-topped clusters of tiny flowers—white and showy in summer—provide pollen for the honeybees. Later on, the purple-black berries furnish food for birds, white-footed mice, even deer, and if we get there in time, excellent pies and jellies for us. Elderberry bushes, easily started by transplanting young shoots, often grow in damp soil, but they also thrive in full sunshine.

Though somewhat more aggressive than the elderberry, some bramble berries such as the raspberry and blackberry should be planted. These can be put in rows and managed, or left to grow on their own into a thicket. The latter is preferred by brown thrashers and catbirds which often nest in the dense canes. The berries ripen in the summer and are extremely attractive to many songbirds and animals, among them the raccoon who will spend many nights in blackberry patches gorging himself on the tasty fruits. In addition, the berries make delicious pies, jellies, and juice. Both blackberries and raspberries can be easily transplanted from the wild.

If there is room, some larger fruit-bearing trees should be planted: crab apples, persimmons, pawpaws, wild plums, and wild black cherries. The wild cherry is a major source of food for wildlife throughout late summer, and the somewhat tart cherries make a superb jelly.

The mulberry is also a good choice, for its berries too are eaten by a host of different birds, and it will help to draw the birds away from cultivated berries.

Another excellent wildlife tree is the serviceberry (*Amelanchier Canadensis*), which is sometimes called Juneberry for the month in which its tangy red berries ripen. This tree is a favorite of ours because it is the first to bloom in the spring on our farm, usually around mid-April, and, according to local lore, signals the proper time to sow oats.

Of course, some nut trees should be added to the planting: the shell-barked or shag-barked hickory, hazelnut, black walnut, and chestnut. A white oak can be planted, along with some evergreens.

The evergreens should be spaced fairly close to each other in order to form a dense cover that offers nesting security and maybe even more important, protection during severe winter weather.

We have a blue spruce not too far from our bird feeders, and practically all the juncos, tree and song sparrows, and cardinals that visit the feeders spend the winter nights within its protective boughs. Last spring pairs of cardinals, mourning doves, robins, song, and chipping sparrows nested in the spruce tree, all at the same time. They likely wouldn't have tolerated others of their own kind, but since all the pairs were of different species they got along peacefully. The cardinals and robins had their nests close to the top of the eighteen-foot-high tree. The mourning doves occupied the center, and the sparrows nested at about eye level.

The best choices in evergreens are the eastern white pine, the Canadian hemlock, and the blue spruce.

The white pine has long three- to five-inch, soft needles and can reach heights of over seventy-five feet. It is a much more attractive tree than the faster-growing Scotch pine with its short, stiff needles. The Canadian hemlock can be planted as a hedge and trimmed back to the desired height. If left to grow, these trees can reach a height of sixty feet or more. The seeds within their three-quarter-inch cones are eaten by some northern birds like the white-winged crossbills and pine grosbeaks. Unlike the pines and hemlocks, blue spruces should be planted as individuals if they are to provide optimum habitat for birds. These spruces branch out from the ground up and, if crowded, tend to become misshapen.

Last but not least, some vines should be encouraged. A vine that is detested by some woodlot owners and the State Forestry Association but is one of our most dependable natural foods for wildlife is the native wild grape. Nearly every bird and animal in the farm woodlot will make a meal of these musky-tasting fruits. As with domestic grapes, wild grapes can easily be propagated by removing a three-bud cutting from the current year's growth and pushing it into the soil so that only one bud remains above ground. Though the wild grape may not be suitable for a backyard, one of the tough tame varieties, such as the Concord, can be planted in a wildlife area and left to grow up a tree with fairly good results. This suits the possums just fine as it seems they prefer Concords to wild grapes. I discovered this a few years ago when I noticed that something was eating our grapes and leaving neat piles of skins on the ground. The mystery was solved several mornings later when our dog barked "treed" on the grape arbor. There, seeking refuge in the bird feeder, was the grape thief—an overweight grinner.

A vine that is somewhat better suited to the backyard is the bittersweet. The flavor of bittersweet makes it somewhat unappetizing to wildlife while there is more favored fare available. But let a long, persistent snowfall cover the main foods of the animals, and the orange-red berries will disappear in short order. Bluebirds, especially, feed on them during severely cold weather. Such emergency foods are just as important as more preferred fare. Bittersweet can be started from cuttings or ordered from some seed catalogs.

To grow a sanctuary from seedlings takes time. But time has a way of going faster than you realize, and before you're aware of it you'll be rewarded hundredfold for your efforts.

Winter
Bird Feeding

There is an old Norwegian tradition of putting a sheaf of grain out for the birds at Christmas time. This sheaf of oats or wheat was cut stem by stem with the farmer's jackknife during the summer as he checked to see if his field was ready to harvest. The stems were tied together into a golden bundle, and this first harvest was then stored to be brought out for the birds on Christmas day. This custom is still practiced in parts of the upper midwest by descendants of Scandinavian settlers.

Many of us, though, feed the birds not only on Christmas, but keep food out for them throughout the winter months. Feeding birds, for us, is rewarding and results in satisfaction as we observe and study the habits of the birds frequenting the feeders by our windows. Not only do we see our resident birds, but also migrants such as the red-breasted nuthatch, black-capped chickadees, slate-colored juncos, and tree sparrows. Occasionally, evening grosbeaks, pine siskins, and common redpolls have made an appearance. We'd miss out on these colorful northern visitors if we didn't maintain well-stocked bird feeders.

It is late October or early November before we begin putting out sunflower seeds and filling the suet and thistle feeders. Once begun, feeding must continue until spring, because feeding attracts more birds to your yard or farm than the natural food supply would support. And when birds come to be dependent upon your feeding them, they should never be deserted, especially not in the middle of winter.

Feeders need not be fancy or elaborate to attract birds. Our main feeder is made out of rough-sawn boards and is about two feet long with solid ends and a two-sided roof. Two-inch-high strips along each side prevent the seeds from blowing out. The reason for having both sides open is that when a timid bird such as a song sparrow or titmouse is inside feeding on sunflowers and a boisterous blue jay comes to claim his share, the smaller bird can escape out the opposite side.

No doubt the most popular bird feed is sunflower seeds. Two types are available—the black-striped (common) sunflower and the smaller oil (black) sunflower. Some birds, like the blue jays and titmice, seem to prefer the striped ones, whereas many of the other birds go for the oil sunflowers. We like to mix the two, about half and half. This seems to satisfy even the most finicky seed eaters.

Then, of course, we have a thistle feeder for the finches and, more rarely, the pine siskins. These cylinders of clear plastic have six tiny openings with perches. It is not unusual to see a goldfinch on each perch feeding on the tiny niger thistle seeds. These feeders are easy to maintain as they need to be refilled only once a week or so, depending on the number of finches feeding. Though the finches go first for thistle seed, they will also feed on the oil sunflower seeds, for which similar feeders are also available.

I've been asked a number of times what can be done about house finches hogging thistle feeders meant for goldfinches. (The house finch is often mistaken for the similar-looking purple finch.) One solution is to cut the perches on the tube feeders back to one-half inch in length. The goldfinch will still perch on the shortened dowel. However, the clumsier house finch will go for a spin.

To cut down on the more expensive seeds, like white proso millet, we scatter cracked corn on the ground. This is simply shelled yellow corn that is put through the feed grinder at a low speed. The cracked corn is attractive to many different species of birds, once the ground is covered with snow. (The snow should be shoveled away or packed down before the cracked corn is spread.) We've had dozens of mourning doves, along with tree and song sparrows and juncos, all feeding at one time. During the night, cottontail rabbits also feast on the corn and so, in turn, leave our young blueberry bushes alone.

Woodpeckers and some other insect-eating birds choose suet over any other food. Unrendered beef suet can be put into mesh onion or orange bags or into holders made from chicken netting and suspended from a tree limb. This is important because cats like suet too, and having these predators around bird feeders is undesirable.

To make another inexpensive feeder, take a piece of wood three or four inches in diameter, cut it about twice the length of a piece of firewood, drill one-inch holes at four-inch intervals through the wood, then drill smaller holes into which sticks are inserted to be used as perches. Drive a fence staple or screw an eyelet into the top end so it can be hung from a limb. Fill these openings with a mixture of peanut butter (plain or crunchy) and cornmeal. Chickadees, titmice, and juncos clean it out in a hurry. Last year our first-grader made one of these as a school project. He tacked the bottom of a bleach jug to the bottom of his feeder to catch tidbits the birds might otherwise drop and waste. There are many other ways that empty plastic bottles and milk cartons can be converted into useful bird feeders.

Some birds, such as horned larks and snow buntings, will readily take to artificial feeding but will not likely come to a feeder close to a house. During the winters of 1976–77 and 1977–78 we were feeding well over five hundred of these birds of the open country on five gallons of cow feed (ground corn and oats) daily. We kept spreading the feed closer and closer to the barn until we had snow buntings and Lapland longspurs feeding right outside a barn window, not over two feet from our faces. It's not often that we get to see birds from arctic regions this close up. As soon as the snow melted, every bird was gone. However, shortly afterward on a Sunday forenoon while we were in church it started snowing, and by the time we got home the ground was covered with several inches of new snow. In the field by the barn hundreds of snow buntings and horned larks were patiently waiting for their handout. We've had some snow buntings several winters since, but not nearly so many as we had through those severe winters.

Anyone who is really serious about feeding birds should buy bird feed in large quantities. Our local feed mill has sunflowers available in fifty-pound bags and niger thistle seed in bulk for a fraction of the cost smaller amounts sell for at the grocery store. It's good to have ample amounts of seeds on hand because more birds might be using the feeders than you realize, as one bird bander discovered. He thought there were about a dozen chickadees visiting his feeder. When he began banding them, he found that there were over a hundred of them.

Perhaps it's difficult for some people to understand why bird feeding can be so enjoyable, yet for many it's not hard to understand at all. Perhaps the pleasure comes from looking for the unexpected visitor—a white-winged crossbill or a pine grosbeak. But even if the rare bird doesn't appear, the many others are there to be enjoyed.

I made a visit to my former schoolteacher on a winter day some years back. He was in his eighties and unable to leave home, but, as I expected, he still had his keen interest in nature and was still feeding the birds. Before I left he told me, "Of all the birds, I have one favorite. It's the song sparrow. Even on the coldest, most blustery days this cheerful bird sits by my window and sings its melodious song. I enjoy it so much. You know, when I was in better health and could go away, I was too busy to notice."

Giving the
Birds a Hand

In our orchard a slowly dying Baldwin apple tree houses a nice woodpecker-made nesting cavity in one of its dead branches. Every spring there is fierce rivalry for the nest site between a pair of northern flickers (who, unlike most woodpeckers, will reuse old nesting holes) and what seems like an endless number of starlings. Without fail the winner is always the starling, an extremely aggressive cavity-nester.

More than forty kinds of birds, not counting the woodpecker, build nests in natural tree cavities, abandoned woodpecker holes, and man-made nesting boxes. This number includes the wood duck, kestrel, and screech owl, in addition to thirty or more species of songbirds. While many of these, especially the songbirds, have been hurt by the invasion of starlings and equally aggressive house sparrows, the eastern bluebird has suffered the most. As the starling took over the bluebird's orchards and fence lines, the house sparrow found its niche around the homesteads.

Of course other factors were involved in the bluebird's demise, including the change from traditional livestock farming to continuous row-crop grain farming, the use of steel fence posts, and pesticides. By 1950 about ninety percent of the bluebird population had been lost. The gentle, soft-voiced bird was no longer considered a harbinger of spring, for few people had seen it or heard its sweet song.

During the last several decades, however, the bluebird population has greatly increased. Thanks to the efforts of many dedicated people who build and maintain bluebird houses, the bluebird is again a fairly common bird in many parts of the East and Midwest. Other cavity-nesting birds, hard-pressed by the competition for homes, have also benefited from the abundance of man-made housing, particularly the tree swallow, but also the tufted titmouse, the Carolina chickadee, and the house wren.

Bluebirders have learned a great deal in recent years about the types of houses that bluebirds prefer. Of the several models of bluebird houses in popular use—among them the North American Bluebird Society House, Hill Lake Bluebird House, and the Peterson Minnesota Bluebird House—each probably has its advantages. Here in Ohio the favorite is one designed by Ohioan Richard Tuttle, called the Tuttle Bluebird House. Almost all of the popular bluebird house designs follow a similar pattern, with the exception of the Peterson Minnesota Bluebird House, which tapers at the bottom.

The boxes we make measure roughly five inches by five inches square and ten inches high. The entrance hole is one and a half inches in diameter and seven and three-fourths inches above the floor. An entrance one and a half inches across will allow other cavity-nesting birds like chickadees, titmice, and tree swallows to enter, while keeping out the starling and the parasitic brown-headed cowbird.

The front of the Tuttle House is designed so that birders can check on its occupants and can clean the house easily. We attach the front a quarter of an inch below the top of the birdhouse for ventilation, which also leaves us a nice quarter-inch handhold at the bottom. To provide additional ventilation and water drainage, we drill four quarter-inch holes through the bottom board.

When the bluebird house is finished, we paint or stain it a

dull color. Never use white—it attracts the unwelcome house sparrow. Bluebirds may shy away from brightly colored boxes. Our neighbor once bought a bluebird house that was painted a brilliant fluorescent orange. While we were threshing wheat at his farm, I noticed the box, which stood out like a cardinal in a flock of snow buntings, and asked him if bluebirds nested in it. "No," he said and chuckled. "Even the house sparrows are afraid to go near it."

We use a dark brown stain on our birdhouses. The linseed oil base gives excellent protection from the weather, and the brown color blends in nicely with the natural environment.

We have learned over the years not to attach bluebird houses directly to wooden fence posts or trees, as this leaves nesting birds vulnerable to predators, primarily domestic cats. All our boxes are now mounted on one-inch steel pipes about five feet above the ground and facing anywhere in the ninety-degree arc from east to south.

Bluebirds raise two or three broods of three to six young each year. During the peak of the nesting season we try to check the boxes at least once a week. Usually I open the box and peer inside to see what is going on, but some bluebirders use a machinist's mirror and a small flashlight to look through the entrance hole. If I find a house sparrow's nest, I remove it. If bluebird nestlings are present, I look for blowfly maggots, particularly in second and third broods. If they aren't controlled, the bloodsucking maggots can kill young bluebirds. The parasites hide on or near the floor of the box and can be rolled out. In heavy infestations the nest can be lightly dusted with rotenone, a natural insecticide that eliminates the pests. If chickadees or tree swallows have taken up housekeeping, I quietly close the box and continue on my way.

Tree swallows had never nested on our farm in numbers until last year, when three pairs nested in our bluebird houses. The pretty green-above-white-below swallow is the first of the swallows to venture north in the spring. Hardier than the others, it will feed on dried berries if the weather is too cold for flying insects. This spring we saw the year's first on Saint Patrick's Day. I was spreading manure when I saw it flying around a bluebird house by the heifer pasture, where a pair of swallows had nested the year before. During the previous fall the heifers had ripped the top off of the Tuttle House, and the swallow had seemed confused. On my next trip past I brought a new box from the shop and replaced the topless one. Getting back on the spreader, I traveled about a hundred feet, stopped the team, and watched as the swallow circled the box several times and then alighted on the top. He inspected his new apartment from different angles, then flew to the front and disappeared through the hole. I went on my way with a warm feeling on a cold March day.

Tree swallows are more aggressive than bluebirds and may eventually take over a house. Many bluebirders in tree swallow country are now placing two houses about seven yards apart, with entrances facing each other. Although bluebirds will not tolerate another pair of their own kind at such close range, and tree swallows will not put up with another pair of swallows, the two species will accept one another as neighbors. Tree swallows will also help in chasing the pesky house sparrows away from the bluebirds.

Now that the tree swallows have settled here, five of the six swallows native to the eastern United States nest regularly on our farm. Though they don't all nest in houses, we can assist them in other ways. For the barn and cliff swallows, we provide two-inch-wide strips of wood for use as nesting ledges. For the rough-winged swallows along the creek, we bore burrows three inches across by two feet deep into the creek bank. The rough-wings build their twig nests and raise their young in these holes.

The purple martins, the largest of the swallows, are almost

totally dependent on man-made housing. Long before European settlers arrived in this country, Native Americans were attracting martins to their homes by hanging hollowed-out gourds on trees and poles. Gourds are still used by some martin enthusiasts, especially in the Southeast, but most martin houses are now built of wood or aluminum.

We are partial to wooden houses because the martins seem to prefer them, and because we can build them ourselves. Ours are octagonal, with sliding fronts for easy cleaning. The entrance holes are one and seven-eighths inches in diameter instead of the recommended two and a quarter inches. The smaller-sized hole prevents owls from preying on the martins. Usually it is the small screech owl that causes problems, but in one case I heard about, a great horned owl was raiding a martin colony. One evening the owl couldn't wait until dark, and as he landed on the house he was greeted with a blast from the farmer's sixteen-gauge shotgun. That put an end to the raider.

There is speculation that the abundant great horned owl may be preying upon another cavity-nesting bird, the barn owl. Ornithologists are somewhat puzzled by the decline of the once common barn owl, and wildlife biologists are now encouraging farmers and other people with suitable buildings to put up nesting boxes for these monkey-faced owls. The nesting boxes are easy to make. The box is forty inches long by sixteen inches high and twelve inches deep. Only a top, bottom, back, and ends are needed because the siding of the barn serves as the front of the box. Place the box on a beam fairly high up and fasten it tightly against the inside of the siding. Then cut a six-inch by nine-inch entrance in the barn siding toward one end of the box. It is advisable to hinge the top so that if pigeons use the box their nest litter can be cleaned out. It is especially important to keep the box pigeon-free in late winter and early spring when barn owls are seeking nesting sites.

Sometimes barn owl nesting boxes are successful, but at

one farm I know of, they did more harm than good. A pair of barn owls nested in a neighbor's barn for three consecutive summers and successfully fledged from five to seven young owls each year. On one Sunday during the second summer, the farm family held church services in the barn. The farmer, who is also the bishop of the church, worried a bit that the extra activity might disturb the young owls. As the congregation filled the benches he would periodically glance at the double beams near the peak of the barn where the nest was located. There was no sign of unrest until the congregation started singing. Then the heads of seven owlets popped above the beam, stretching this way and that, eyes blinking to see what in the world was going on. But my friend soon relaxed, because shortly after the preacher began his sermon the owls went back to sleep, awakening only at the closing hymn.

Some time later, a conservation group found out about the barn owls and, with noble intentions, put up a nesting box on the beams. The owls left and never returned.

Human "assistance" rarely brings about such negative results. As I write this I listen to the pleasing chatter of the purple martins and the barn and cliff swallows through the screen door. In the distance I hear the song of the bluebird. These birds are here, I like to think, because we help them.

DAVID KLINE was born on the family farm where he has lived for more than fifty years. With his wife Elsie and their children, and the help of his neighbors and horses, David practices diversified sustainable farming and is a member of the Amish community in North central Ohio. He is also the author of *Scratching the Woodchuck: Nature On an Amish Farm* and is currently editor of the magazine *Farming: People, Land, and Community*.